Birth of a Legend: The Spitfire

Birth of a Legend: The Spitfire

Jeffrey Quill

OBE, AFC, FRAeS

with Sebastian Cox MA

Foreword by
Air Vice-Marshal J.E. 'Johnnie' Johnson
CB, CBE, DSO and two Bars, DFC and Bar

SMITHSONIAN INSTITUTION PRESS
Washington D.C.

Acknowledgements

The authors gratefully acknowledge the substantial help received from a number of sources in the preparation of this book. In particular our thanks go to Air Vice-Marshal J.E. Johnson, CB, CBE, DSO and two bars, DFC and bar, for so kindly agreeing to write the foreword, and to Air Marshal Sir Humphrey Edwardes Jones, KCB, CBE, DFC, AFC, BA, for his assistance with the chapter on the production order. Mr Alan Clifton, lately Head of the Supermarine Technical Office; Messrs Jack Rice and Jack Davis, late of the Supermarine Design Department; Mr Alec Harvey-Bailey, late of Rolls Royce Limited and Mr Michael Evans, Chairman of the Rolls-Royce Heritage Trust, were all immensely helpful.

We are also indebted to Mr Alec Lumsden for his invaluable help in assembling the photographs and writing many of the captions. Our thanks also go to Mr Peter Pimblett, the Royal Aeronautical Society, the Imperial War Museum, Joe Merchant of Circuit Publications, and the Quadrant Picture Library, for access to their photographic collections, and to the Royal Air Force Museum, Hendon, for their invaluable help with both photographic and documentary material.

Mr Frank Wootton, Mr Gerald Coulson, Mr Alan Fearnley and Mr Roger Steel all kindly gave us permission to reproduce, in colour, their magnificent oil paintings. We also gratefully acknowledge the help received from Dr N.A. Barfield and Messrs C.F. Andrews and E.B. Morgan, all of British Aerospace. We are especially grateful to Air Commodore Henry Probert, MBE, MA, Head of the Air Historical Branch of the Ministry of Defence, for the substantial help and encouragement received from that quarter.

Last but by no means least our thanks go to Miss Liz Lawrence, who typed almost the entire manuscript.

*PUBLISHED IN ASSOCIATION WITH
BRITISH AEROSPACE PLC AND ROLLS-ROYCE LIMITED*

Published in the United States of America by
SMITHSONIAN INSTITUTION PRESS

First published by
Quiller Press Ltd
50 Albermarle Street,
London W.1.

First published 1986
Second impression 1986

ISBN 87474 776 7
Library of Congress no: 86 60544

Designed by Jim Reader

Design and production in association with
Book Production Consultants, Cambridge

Typeset and printed by The Burlington Press (Cambridge) Ltd, Foxton

Contents

Foreword

by Air Vice-Marshal 'Johnnie' Johnson

My old friend, Jeffrey Quill, spent much of his time with the fighter squadrons — flying with us, discussing ideas and tactics and sorting out any snags with our Spitfires. One of our problems was with fabric ailerons which made the Spitfire almost uncontrollable in a steep dive, but in early 1941 Jeffrey told us that metal-skinned ailerons were available which greatly reduced the previous heavy stick-pressures and the rate of roll at high speed was more than doubled. If we could get our Spitfires to Hamble, said Jeffrey, the new ailerons could be immediately fitted.

Our wing leader was the legendary Douglas Bader and naturally his Spitfire was the first to have the new ailerons fitted, and a day or so later we bounced a gaggle of Messerschmitts over St. Omer. The Messerschmitts evaded by half-rolling and diving steeply. Bader dived after them leaving the rest of the squadron, with our fabric ailerons, trying unsuccessfully to stay with him; our squadron commander, Billy Burton, called his superior officer to order: "Douglas, we cannot keep up – we haven't all got bloody metal ailerons."

The Whitehall bureaucracy caught up towards the end of 1942 when I received an offical letter demanding an explanation as to why 616 Squadron had fitted metal ailerons without proper authority. Who had authorised the work at Hamble? And who was going to pay? I replied that since I was only a Pilot Officer at the time I could throw no light on the matter but doutless Wing Commander Douglas Bader could fully explain and he could be contacted at Stalag Luft III!

I did not get my hands on the beautiful Spitfire IX, with its new 1600 hp Merlin 61 engine, until I led the Canadian Spitfire Wing from Kenley in the spring of 1943. Jeffrey has fully described the Spitfire IX and its great tactical advantage was that except for its longer nose and more exhaust stubs, it looked exactly like the inferior Spitfire V. In the air the Germans did not know the difference until we had hit them.

My own regret about the Spitfire was its lack of range. In 1943 wing leaders, like me, felt very badly because we did not have the range to escort the Fortresses on their daily bombing raids over Germany and they suffered heavy casualties until the Mustangs came along and escorted the Fortresses to Berlin and back.

Our Spitfires had their main armament in their wings and the only space for extra internal tankage was in the fuselage behind the pilot, which resulted in a large rearward movement of the centre of gravity and so caused considerable stability problems which, however, were on their way to solution when the war ended.

There is no doubt that the Spitfire IX was the finest defensive fighter of its era and here is what some of our great fighter pilots had to say about this beautiful aeroplane:

"It was always a delight to fly, was supremely responsive to the controls at all speeds in all attitudes of flight and, with all this, a very stable gun platform."
'Dutch' Hugo (South Africa)

"I only flew Spitfires in combat. No mean feat. I grew to envy the Mustang's great range, however."
Rod Smith (Canada)

"I flew most of the various marks of Spitfires, but I felt sort of invincible in the Spitfire IX."
Larry Robillard (Canada)

"The Spitfire was an incredible, immortal combat vehicle."
Danforth Browne (U.S.A.)

"I preferred the Spitfire to other fighters because it had few vices. It was fast, very manoeuverable and had a high rate of climb."
Pat Jameson (New Zealand)

"The versatility and the deceptive toughness of this fighter made it, I think without question, the outstanding fighter aircraft of the Second World War."
Al Deere (New Zealand)

"The aircraft was part of you and, when frightened, either in testing or in combat, I think one used to talk to one's Spitfire, and you may be equally sure that it used to answer."
Paddy Barthropp (U.K.)

"Because I lost my second and third log books, I do not know exactly how many hours I flew a Spitfire altogether, but it must have been about 2,000, of which at least half must have been on operations. The Spitfire never let me down."
'Cocky' Dundas (U.K.)

Preface

This book is not unique, no book about the Spitfire could be that. It is not even a history of the aircraft, or of the operations in which Spitfires took part. It is rather, as the title suggests, the story of the birth of a legend, for no other aircraft has ever had quite the charisma, almost a mystical aura, that the name Spitfire can evoke in both young and old. If you sit near to the Spitfires on display in the Royal Air Force Museum at Hendon, you will see large numbers of small boys pass by the others famous aircraft nearby with only a cursory glance, but they invariably stop to gaze at the slender lines of R.J. Mitchell's masterpiece.

This book does not take the story much beyond the Battle of Britain. Its concern is with the men and the organisations behind the legend; those people who laboured long and hard to design and build the aircraft for others to fly. The many, largely unsung, heroes in Supermarine, Vickers and Rolls-Royce, who were able to take the undoubted genius of Mitchell's original design, and turn it into a triumph of a different sort – a triumph of production and sustained development. The quite extraordinary success of the production programme, which saw a grand total of 22,759 Spitfires and Seafires built, is all the more commendable when the size of the aircraft industry in 1936, and the initial problems with production are taken into account. Equally worthy of the highest praise are the achievements of Mitchell's successor at Supermarine, Joseph Smith, and his assistants, together with the design team at Rolls-Royce under Ernest Hives, who successfully developed both airframe and engines to levels undreamt of by R.J. Mitchell in the early thirties. Their success kept the Spitfire at the forefront of piston-engined fighter development throughout the war.

Fundamentally the legend was established by the skill and courage of the fighter pilots who flew the aircraft in action, and by the fact that the Spitfire, together with the Hurricane, enabled RAF Fighter Command to achieve a vital feat of arms in the summer of 1940 which lifted the morale and spirit of the British people at a time of desperate need. But the skill and courage of the pilots would all have been for naught without the dedication of those behind the scenes. The maintenance crews, the designers, the draughtsmen, the production managers, and the men and women who put the aircraft together, as well as the men of vision and courage at all levels in the various ministries. These men and women were the midwives to the legend.

Jeffrey Quill
Sebastian Cox

London October 1985

CHAPTER 1

Backdrop

The Vickers Supermarine Spitfire, powered with its Rolls-Royce Merlin engine, was destined to become one of the most illustrious and famous fighter aircraft of all time.

It first flew, in prototype form, on 5 March 1936, at Eastleigh airport near Southampton. The test pilot was Joseph Summers — 'Mutt' Summers to all his friends and colleagues in the aviation world.

The Supermarine Aviation Works at Woolston, Southampton, was at that time a wholly owned subsidiary of Vickers Ltd, the great British shipbuilding, engineering and armament company. It comprised, in all its many establishments and subsidiaries throughout the country, some 80,000 employees.

At this time the aviation interests of Vickers were vested in Vickers (Aviation) Ltd at Weybridge, Surrey, who also controlled the Supermarine Aviation Works at Southampton which had been bought by Vickers in 1928. The Supermarine Aviation Works was a small firm in those days — under 1,000 employees — which after its foundation in 1913 by Noel Pemberton Billing had, from the latter part of World War I, specialized in the design and construction of flying boats, and had then sprung to international fame through the series of its racing seaplanes which won Schneider Trophy Contests and set up world speed records.

The Rolls-Royce company, internationally famous for its magnificent motor-cars which had long been synonymous with superlative engineering, reliability and luxurious excellence, had during World War I turned its attention to the design and manufacture of aeroplane engines. It produced some highly successful engines for military aircraft and continued in the aero-engine field after the war, supplying engines for the Royal Air Force and for the emergent civil aviation requirements of the 1920s.

However, after the First War times were hard and little money was available to industry for the design and development of new aircraft or engines. Engines of later design, such as the Napier Lion and Bristol Jupiter, began to displace the Rolls-Royce products and business was on the wane. Furthermore there were elements in the Board Room of the Rolls-Royce head office in Conduit Street who wanted the energies of the company to be devoted to motor-cars rather than aero engines.

It was in the mid-1920s, when the Fairey Aviation Company obtained a licence to manufacture the successful Curtiss D.12 liquid-cooled engine from America, that Sir Henry Royce was inspired to design the F.10 which was to become the Kestrel. This engine of V.12 liquid-cooled layout set Rolls-Royce on a course of post-war engine development which was to lead to great things in the future.

By the mid-1930s the other main British aero-engine companies were Bristol and Armstrong Siddeley, who had concentrated on air-cooled radial layouts, and Napier who, like Rolls-Royce, had concentrated primarily upon liquid-cooled engines. De Havilland produced a series of smaller but very successful civil engines.

By 1936, when the Spitfire made its first flight, the Royal Air Force was in the early stages of a series of expansion programmes which had been started by the Government, somewhat belatedly, as the threat from Hitler's Nazi Germany became increasingly apparent from 1934 onwards. This simultaneously produced the need for rapid expansion of the British aircraft and engine industries in design, development, and manufacturing capacity.

In 1918, at the end of World War I, the Royal Air Force was the largest air force in the world, supported by the largest aircraft industry. Inevitably during the 1920s both were run down to a shadow of their former selves and by the mid-1930s the Royal Air Force's equipment had become somewhat out of date. Furthermore the Service itself was neither structured nor geared for the possibility of a European war, for since the end of World War I its principal roles and activities had been overseas in Britain's Imperial possessions.

So very considerable and radical changes were needed, and not only was industry required to produce many more engines, aeroplanes and pieces of equipment to implement the RAF's expansion programmes, but great technological strides were simultaneously needed to make their performance and military capabilities consistent with the requirements of a major European war.

The depredations of what Winston Churchill called 'the locust years' had to be made good — and quickly. So in the mid-1930s technology and output were the simultaneous challenges facing the aircraft industry and it was against this background that the Supermarine Spitfire and the Rolls-Royce Merlin engine were designed from 1933–4 onwards.

Beginnings

In 1913 Noel Pemberton Billing, a man who might fairly be described as an adventurous and active-minded eccentric, formed a company for the purpose of designing and building flying boats or, as he conceived it, boats that flew rather than aeroplanes that floated. He established Works at Woolston on the River Itchen, near Southampton, adjacent to a yacht basin which he already owned. In 1914 the firm became a limited company — Pemberton Billing Ltd — with a nominal capital of £20,000 with Alfred de Broughton as co-subscriber.

Pemberton Billing's first flying boat was the PB1 which was exhibited at the Olympia Aero Show of March 1914, but it is doubtful whether the PB1 ever actually flew. When World War I broke out he built a small single-seat scout aircraft, the PB9, said to have been designed and built in nine days, which however did not go into production. The company then concentrated upon Admiralty aircraft repair and overhaul work. Pemberton Billing

Pemberton Billing's original Woolston Works

LEFT: *The first Super-marine aircraft: Pember-ton Billing with the PB1 at Olympia in 1914. It is uncertain whether or not this machine actually flew*

BELOW LEFT: *The PB25 first flew in September 1915. After test and de-velopment flying some 20 examples of this aircraft were built, but owing to engine problems it never went into service*

BELOW: *The N1 Baby. This was the first Super-marine aircraft on which R. J. Mitchell is known to have worked, under the su-pervision of F. J. Har-greaves. It also established a tradition of small single-engined amphibious flying boats at Supermarine*

also designed and built a small single-seat pusher scout, the PB25, which went into limited production but never saw operational service. Also an order was secured from the Admiralty for twelve Short S.38 dual-control training aircraft.

Several other projects were undertaken during those early days and examination of the company's activities shows a bias towards marine aircraft, the Admiralty rather than the War Office being their principal customer.

In 1916 Pemberton Billing left to become an MP and control of the company passed to Hubert Scott-Paine as Managing Director and, on 20 September 1916, the company was re-registered as the Supermarine Aviation Works. At about this stage the firm was receiving work from the Admiralty Air Department who pro-duced original project designs which were then passed to selected firms to complete the detail design and construct prototypes and, in some cases, production versions. The Admiralty Air Depart-ment, under the control of Rear Admiral Sir Murray Sueter, was becoming technically more sophisticated and started to lay down formalized design and construction standards to be observed by contractors. Thus the company formally entered the design field.

Supermarine worked on a number of these A.D. designs, as they were called, and one of them led to the building of a small single-seat pusher wooden-hulled biplane flying boat called the N.1. 'Baby'. This flew quite successfully, with two different types

of engine tried in succession. With a 200 hp Hispano-Suiza engine it had a top speed of 116 mph and a duration of three hours.

A Fleet Air Arm Walrus being hoisted on to the catapult of a cruiser

This little aircraft is of considerable significance for various reasons: firstly, its operational concept was as a naval single-seater fighter — thus the first-ever flying-boat fighter. Secondly, it established a formula for small single-engined biplane amphibious flying boats which Supermarine were to develop successfully in the future through the Sea Lion, which won the Schneider Trophy in 1922 at Naples, the Seagulls for the Royal Australian Navy and the Royal Air Force and then the never-to-be-forgotten Walrus for the Royal Navy and the RAF Air-Sea Rescue Service in World War II, and later still the Sea Otter.

Thirdly, but perhaps most important of all, is that working on the design of the N.1. 'Baby' under the supervision of F.J. Hargreaves was a young draughtsman and technician called Reginald Joseph Mitchell.

CHAPTER 3

R.J. Mitchell and early projects

R. J. Mitchell

The P31E Zeppelin-destroyer. This remarkably futuristic design, equipped with a gimbal-mounted searchlight, an internal auxiliary power unit and an upper gun mounting, never actually went into service. Mitchell is known to have worked on the detail design

R.J. Mitchell was born in 1895, the eldest son of Herbert Mitchell of Calke near Stoke-on-Trent. He was educated at Hanley Grammar School and served an engineering apprenticeship with Kerr Stuart & Co, builders of steam locomotives. He extended the scope of his studies to engineering drawing, mechanics and higher mathematics by attending night school.

In 1916, at the age of twenty-one, Mitchell was engaged by Pemberton Billing Ltd as a draughtsman to do design work and strength calculations. It was Hubert Scott-Paine, then Manager of the company, who engaged him, although it is not certain how Mitchell came to apply for the job. It is known however that as a boy Mitchell was interested in flying and (like Sydney Camm) spent much time building and flying model aeroplanes. Certainly Scott-Paine could hardly have appreciated at the time the enormous impact upon the future of the new and immature company which his decision to engage Mitchell was to have.

Pemberton Billing had been dedicated to the production of maritime aircraft, believing that that was where the future of aviation lay, but the requirements of war made it necessary that some land-planes were built. Notable among these was a pair of very large quadruplanes, the P29E and P31E. These were designed by Pemberton Billing to meet an Admiralty requirement for a Zeppelin-destroyer. The crew were enclosed within a glazed cabin, there was a gun turret above the upper mainplane intended

to mount a cannon and at the nose of the aircraft was a gimbal-mounted searchlight powered by an internally mounted auxiliary power unit.

It is known that the young R.J. Mitchell worked on the detail design of this remarkably futuristic project. The first one, the P29E, crashed early in its trials, but the second, the P31E with two 100 hp Anzani engines, flew fairly successfully at Eastchurch, achieving a top speed of 75 mph and a landing speed of 35 mph. The aircraft was designed to have long patrol endurance and good altitude performance to allow it to lie in wait for Zeppelins, pick them up in its searchlight and destroy them with its heavy-calibre machine-gun. It never went into operational service.

Mitchell's involvement with the N.1. 'Baby' flying boat has already been mentioned and by the time the war ended he had been appointed Chief Designer and Chief Engineer of Supermarine.

Once the war was over the company reverted to its original intention to develop flying boats and it did not depart from this course for several years. The first significant post-war design was the Channel Type flying boat, a development of the wartime A.D. flying boat, and intended for the commercial carriage of passengers. To help create a market for these aircraft Supermarine formed an operating company, starting a passenger service to the Isle of Wight in 1919, and later a service between Southampton and Cherbourg using Channel Type boats.

The Channel Type boat had some commercial sales success, two being sold to an operating company in Norway and some to Venezuela, Brazil, Chile and Japan. Supermarine, in partnership with A.V. Roe and the Beardmore Aero Engine Company, also formed Bermuda and West Atlantic Air Services Ltd. In 1922 Supermarine, continuing its policy of operating air services to stimulate the market for its products, joined with the London and South-Western Railway Company to form the British Marine Air Navigation Company Ltd, and received official permission to operate services between Southampton and the Channel Islands and Southampton and Cherbourg.

Apart from these excursions into commercial passenger-carrying operations the early post-war years are remarkable for the diversity and enterprise of the company's activities in the design and building of experimental flying boats and amphibian prototypes. Much of this spirit of energy and enterprise was due to the arrival in the company of Squadron Commander James Bird, who entered partnership with Scott-Paine in the ownership of the company. This gave great stimulus and commercial drive to Mitchell's restless, inventive and innovative spirit in the design field and resulted in a series of prototypes such as the Martlesham Amphibian of 1920, which was second in an Air Ministry competition and so highly thought of by the judges that the value of the second prize was doubled. This led on to the Seal in 1921, which was later renamed the Seagull and produced for the RAF and RAAF, and also in 1921 the Sea King Mk II, a small military amphibian.

In 1922 a major event was the winning in Naples of the

The Seagull II. 480 hp Napier Lion. This aircraft, originally the Seal, was renamed Seagull in July 1922, and a tacit undertaking was made by the Air Ministry to order 18.

In 1925 the RAAF ordered 6 Seagull IIIs, which differed only in detail from the Seagull II. These were stationed at Point Cook, Victoria, and formed No. 101 Fleet Co-operation Flight RAAF in June 1926

Hubert Scott-Paine

The Sea Eagle. A six-passenger enclosed cabin aircraft built for the air service between Southampton, Le Havre, Cherbourg and the Channel Isles. The engine was a Rolls-Royce Eagle IX

Schneider Trophy for Great Britain at 145 mph with the Sea Lion II with 450 hp Napier Lion engine. This was before the days of Government sponsorship of Schneider Trophy entries and the Sea Lion competed entirely at the expense of the company. Had Henri Biard (the company's test pilot) not won this race the Trophy would have remained permanently in Italy and the competition would have lapsed with unpredictable effects for the future.

The company's interest in producing aircraft for commercial passenger-carrying purposes resulted in 1923 in the Sea Eagle six-passenger commercial amphibian, with a Rolls-Royce Eagle IX engine and a range of 230 miles. Three were built and operated successfully for some years by Imperial Airways.

Then, in 1924, clearly under the influence of the company's interest in the commercial operation of passenger services, Mitchell designed the Swan amphibian, capable of accommodating 12 passengers within the hull and departing for the first time from the single-engine formula, having twin Rolls-Royce Eagle IX engines driving tractor propellers.

So favourable were the results of the official trials of the Swan at the Marine Aircraft Experimental Establishment (MAEE), Felixstowe, that Mitchell was encouraged to design a military version of this essentially civil aeroplane and this led to his design of the Southampton flying boat to Air Ministry specification R28/24.

The Air Ministry took the very unusual step of ordering six of these aircraft straight off the drawing-board. This move was no doubt influenced by the great success of the Swan trials at MAEE, but it must also indicate that by this time Mitchell as a designer had achieved an exceptional degree of standing and the confidence of Air Ministry circles.

The Swan. Mitchell's twin-engined design for a commercial aircraft to carry twelve passengers, with twin Rolls-Royce Eagle IX engines. The success of this aircraft encouraged Mitchell to design a military version with two Napier Lion engines

CHAPTER 4

The 'Southampton' Flying Boat

The Southampton, with two Napier Lion engines of 450 hp each, made its first flight at Woolston on 10 March 1925 in the hands of Henri Biard. In spite of some minor trouble with the wing-tip floats which were later redesigned, the aircraft was flown to Felixstowe for the official tests after only four days of contractor's trials at the Works. Deliveries of production Southamptons to No.480 Coastal Reconnaissance Flight, RAF, at Calshot commenced in the summer of 1925.

Like all previous Supermarine flying boats the Southampton had a wooden hull. These hulls, of double-skinned mahogany diagonal planking with the planing bottom and steps attached separately forming a double bottom, were superb examples of the boatbuilder's craft.* Later however, Mitchell set about the design, to the identical external lines, of a metal hull of light alloy construction. The Southampton was a very efficient aircraft of simple and rugged design with a range of about five hundred miles and carrying a crew of five. Essential maintenance could be carried out by its own crew whilst on a mooring.

The year 1925 was a period when aviation in general was having to struggle to gain public recognition and acceptance. The Royal Air Force in particular, formed only seven years previously in 1918 as the first independent air force in the world, equally was having to struggle for recognition of its strategic potential and to stem a tide of hostility from the older Services and a certain political apathy within the Government.

The Southampton flying boat with its long range, its reliability, ease of maintenance and independence of aerodromes, provided the Air Staff with precisely the vehicle they needed to demonstrate the possibilities of the air and to blaze the trail of future commercial air routes.

A series of cruises by formations of Southamptons was flown. The first was a 20-day cruise of 1,000 miles by four aircraft in formation round the British Isles. Exercises with the Royal Navy in the Irish Sea were carried out en route and the flag was shown at various coastal towns in the north of Ireland and south-west Scotland. Later a single aircraft flew from Felixstowe to Plymouth, thence to Belfast lough via Carrickfergus and on to Oban and across Scotland to Cromarty, the Firth of Forth and back to

---

*A portion of one has survived and after years of service as a garden shed is now being restored for eventual display in the Royal Air Force Museum at Hendon.

Felixstowe. The official communiqué on these cruises finished up by saying, 'Refuelling at sea was carried out on all occasions without a hitch . . . and it has been demonstrated that they [the flying boats], can function successfully quite separately and independently of their land bases.'

The next cruise, a somewhat more ambitious affair, was in July 1926 when two Southamptons under the command of Squadron Leader G.E. Livock, DFC, left Plymouth for Aboukir, Eygpt, via Bordeaux, Marseilles, Naples, Malta and Benghazi, calling at Athens and Corfu on the return flight. This cruise covered a total distance of some 7,000 miles.

Soon after the return of the two boats from Egypt the Air Ministry laid on public demonstration tours by four Southamptons, starting at Cromer on the east coast and visiting most of the east and south coast towns all the way round to Torquay. This was an undisguised public relations exercise done at a time when aircraft of any sort were a great novelty to the public; the large but elegant Southampton flying boats, flying in formation and alighting on the water, created a considerable impression amongst the holiday crowds, who otherwise had little opportunity to see anything of the Royal Air force.

The introduction of the metal hull for the Southampton, which made it into the Southampton II, resulted in nearly 1,000lb saving of weight leading to an increase in the cruising range of the aircraft.

And so in 1928 the largest and most ambitious cruise was organized, known as the Far East Flight. Four metal-hulled Southamptons, under the command of Group Captain H.N.

Southampton MK II. Mitchell's first all-metal hull, identical in form to the Southampton I, this splendid aircraft established Mitchell's reputation as a flying boat designer

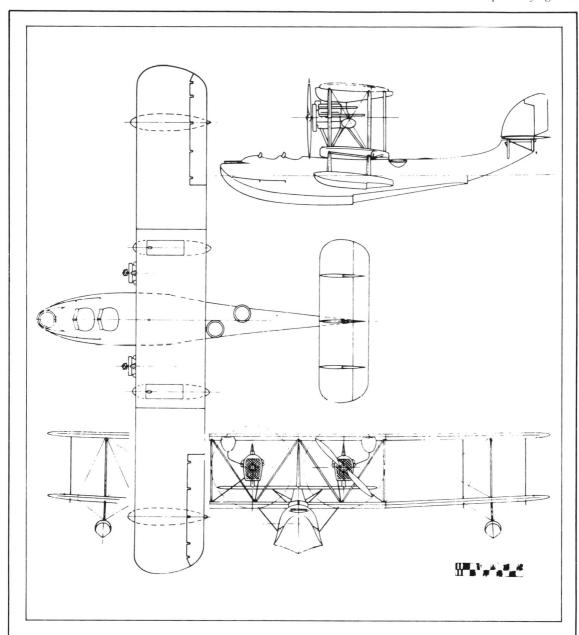

The 'Southampton' flying boat

Cave-Brown-Cave, flew in formation over a distance of 23,000 miles. Starting from Plymouth they crossed Europe, passed through the Mediterranean and across Syria and Iraq, through the Persian Gulf to Karachi and coastwise round India to Calcutta, thence via Rangoon to Singapore. From Singapore they flew to Australia, which they completely circumnavigated coastwise, and then returned to Singapore via New Guinea and Borneo, making a trip to Hong Kong before finally taking up station at Singapore.

Throughout this cruise the aircraft were maintained by their own crews who slept on board at a large number of the stopping-places. There was very little technical trouble and schedules were on the whole closely maintained. No records were broken nor was any attempt made to break any. It was an exercise in unspectacular achievement, reliability and the maintenance of schedules. It had a big effect upon the aviation community at large and particularly upon those whose thoughts were moving towards the opening up of Empire air routes and the commercial carriage of passengers and mail over long distances. This remarkable performance by the Southampton flying boats still further enhanced Mitchell's burgeoning reputation as an aircraft designer.

CHAPTER 5

The S.4 in 1925

It will be remembered that Mitchell's design of a small single-seat flying boat, the Sea Lion II with Napier Lion engine, won the Schneider Trophy at Naples in 1922.

For the 1923 contest, which was to take place at Calshot, Mitchell prepared a cleaned-up and developed version of the Sea Lion called the Sea Lion III, with a more powerful version of the Napier Lion engine in a much improved and aerodynamically cleaner nacelle and a modified hull designed to reduce drag in the air, and wings with span reduced by four feet. Again this entry was without Government financial backing other than the loan of the Sea Lion aircraft to enable Supermarine to modify it and enter it at their own expense.

The United States Navy entered a team consisting of two Curtiss CR.3 biplane floatplanes with 450 hp Curtiss D.12 engines and one Navy Wright biplane with Wright T-2 engine. This US Navy team made 1923 something of a watershed year in the history of the Schneider Trophy Contest. In 1913 Jacques Schneider had believed, rather like Pemberton Billing, that as most of the earth's surface is covered with water the real future of aviation lay with marine aircraft, and accordingly he framed the original rules of his contest in 1913 to encourage the development of this type of aircraft. However as time went on the contest increasingly developed into a pure speed race, and this process was finally clinched by the nature of the American entries of 1923. These were unashamedly pure racing seaplanes making little concession to anything other than speed, and rather naturally they outclassed the Sea Lion III which, when all was said and done, was essentially a flying boat, albeit one of remarkably high performance.

The 1923 race was won by Lieutenant Rittenhouse USN, in a Curtiss CR.3 at a speed of 177.88 mph, which represented a new world air speed record. Lt Irvine, USN, was second at 173.47 mph and Henri Biard was third in the Sea Lion at 157.17 mph.

The effect of this 1923 contest upon R.J. Mitchell was to convince him that henceforth the Schneider aircraft would have to be designed with the achievement of the maximum possible speed as the prime objective, other qualities being given only such consideration as would allow the aircraft to conform with the rules and operate in reasonable safety. In other words future contestants would have to take on a very new look, vastly different from the Sea Lion flying boats.

The Supermarine S.4 was the aircraft which emerged from Woolston Works on 24 August 1925. Technologically it was a

huge stride ahead not only of previous British Schneider entries but also of the American biplane floatplanes which had swept all before them in 1923. It was a twin-float midwing monoplane powered by the well-tried Napier Lion 12-cylinder liquid-cooled engine, in this case uprated to 700 bph and driving a Fairey Reed metal-bladed propeller. The rear fuselage and cockpit sections were of wooden stressed-skin construction and the wing, built as a single unit, was also constructed of wood and covered with ply. A most unusual and bold feature was that the wings and float structures were fully cantilever, having no external wire bracing whatever. The wing was fitted with trailing edge flaps situated inboard of the ailerons, and the ailerons themselves were operated by push-pull rods rather than the more conventional cable and pulley mechanism and were mounted on torque tubes.

The engine was very closely cowled round its three rows of cylinder blocks, the wing roots fairing in behind the outboard blocks.

The Lamblin radiator units were recessed into the lower surface of each wing and represented the only excrescences protruding into the airstream over the whole aircraft.

The S.4, operating from Calshot and flown by Henri Biard, established a world speed record for seaplanes of 226.75 mph over the measured 3 km course in Southampton Water before proceeding to the United States for the 1925 Schneider Trophy Contest.

The rest of the 1925 British team consisted of two Gloster–Napier III biplane floatplanes.

Sadly, while practising for the race at Boston, the S.4 hit the sea when executing a turn and was totally destroyed, Biard somewhat miraculously escaping with his life. The cause of the crash was

ABOVE: *The Supermarine S.4, Mitchell's exceptionally clean and technologically advanced design of 1925, with special Napier Lion engine of 700 hp*

BELOW: *The basic structure was of wood, wings and float structure were fully cantilever. Trailing edge flaps were incorporated to reduce landing and take-off speeds, the ailerons were mounted on torque tubes and the Lamblin radiators for the main engine coolant were semi-recessed within the wings. A Fairey-Reed duralumin propeller was fitted.*

The S.4 established a world speed record for seaplanes on Southampton Water at 226.75 mph, before leaving by Bay Shore, Baltimore, USA for the Schneider contest. Sadly the S.4 crashed while practising for the race, but the pilot, Henri Biard, was uninjured. The cause of the crash was probably wing flutter or aileron reversal. All Mitchell's subsequent Schneider designs were fully wire-braced

The Curtiss R3C 2, winner of the 1925 Schneider Trophy, flown by Lt James Doolittle, US Army

never positively established, but it is probable that it was due either to wing flutter or aileron reversal. Subsequently all Supermarine Schneider racing aircraft reverted to wire-braced wing and float structures.

The 1925 race was won by Lt James Doolittle, US Army, in a Curtiss R3C-2 biplane floatplane at 234.4 mph, with Hubert Broad second, for Britain, in the Gloster III biplane at 199 mph.

However, Mitchell's design of the S.4 had set a pattern and a standard for the future which he was to pursue with outstanding success.

CHAPTER 6

1927 and the S.5

Britain did not enter for the 1926 contest at Hampton Roads (USA), which thus became a straight contest between Italy and USA. Italy won with a new aircraft and engine combination, the Macchi M.39 with 800 hp. Fiat AS2 engine at a speed of 247.8 mph, flown by De Bernardi. The Americans entered slightly developed Curtiss R3C-2 aircraft and Lt Schilt was second in one of these. To the Italians therefore went the distinction of flying the first monoplane floatplane in the history of the contest, a distinction of which Britain had been robbed in 1925 by the crash of Mitchell's S.4 before the race.

After the 1925 race the British Government decided that private industry could no longer be expected to compete alone against Government-sponsored teams such as the US Navy team of 1923, US Army teams of 1925 and 1926 and the Italian teams.

Macchi M.52 competed in the 1927 race at Venice, flown by Captain Arturo Ferrarin. Engine was a 1,000 hp Fiat AS.3

The Gloster – Napier IVB which used the Gloster III design as a starting point

Accordingly it was decided that in future the Royal Air Force would compete on behalf of Britain and the RAF High Speed Flight was formed at Felixstowe to start training for the 1927 race. Three new aircraft were designed for the race, the Supermarine S.5, the Gloster IV, and the Short Crusader, the last having a Bristol Mercury engine. The Crusader had the misfortune (like the S.4) to crash while preparing for the race which was flown in Venice, Italy having won in 1926.

The S.5 won this race at 283.3 mph (453.26 km/h) flown by Flight Lieutenant S.N. Webster; the other S.5, flown by Flight Lieutenant Worsley, was second at 273 mph (486.9 km/h).

BOTTOM: *Supermarine S.5. The Schneider Trophy winner of 1927. Powered with a geared but unsupercharged Napier Lion VIIB engine of 870 hp, it was a fully braced monoplane of composite wood and metal construction. The percentage structure weight of the S.5 was 36% as against the 45% of the S.4. Surface radiators, composed of a double skin covering almost the whole of the upper and lower surfaces of the wing were used in place of the protuberant Lamblin radiators, and the oil coolers were situated down each side of the fuselage – the tank being in the fin.*

The S.5 won the race at 283.3 mph and the other S.5 (with direct drive Napier engine) was second at 273 mph

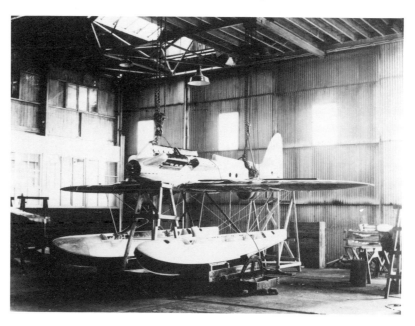

LEFT: *Flt Lieut S. N. Webster crossing the finishing line at Venice to win the 1927 Schneider Trophy*

RIGHT: *S.5 getting up 'on the step'*

Mitchell's S.5 was arguably one of the most efficient racing craft of the whole Schneider series. It was a low-wing monoplane of composite wood and metal construction with (after the experience of the S.4) fully wire-braced wing and float structures. With the elimination of the cantilever wing and float structures the S.5's percentage structure weight was reduced to 36% from the 45% of the S.4. The frontal area of the floats was reduced by 14% by reducing their reserve buoyancy, and the cross-sectional area of the fuselage was reduced by as much as 35%, which necessitated the fuel being carried in the floats.

The protuberant Lamblin radiators of the S.4 were completely eliminated and replaced by double-skinned surface coolers made of copper sheet, situated on the surface of the wings with surface oil coolers at the fuselage sides. Thus cooling drag was reduced to the absolute minimum.

A Napier Lion VIIB engine of 750 bhp was fitted. This was normally aspirated (unsupercharged) but had the then very high compression ratio of 10/1 which necessitated the use of a special fuel mixture, 75% gasoline, 23% Benzole and 2% tetraethyl lead.

Mitchell's S.5 was one of the most efficient of all the racing seaplanes designed during the history of the Schneider contests. Dr. Ing. Ermanno Bazzocchi of Aeronautica Macchi described it as 'near optimum' for aircraft confined to engines of less than 1,000 hp. But the state of the art achieved in 1927 indicated that if speeds were to be increased much further very large increases in available horse-power would be necessary in the future.

Between the 1927 and 1929 races an event of the utmost significance for Supermarine took place. The company was bought by Vickers Aviation Ltd, a wholly owned subsidiary of Vickers Ltd, the great engineering, shipbuilding and armament company. The Chairman of Vickers Aviation Ltd was the shrewd

LEFT: *Macchi M.52s at Venice, 1927*

and farseeing Sir Robert McLean who, although accountable to the main Board of Vickers Ltd for the conduct of the Aviation Company, none the less operated with a high degree of autonomy and independence.

By the purchase of the Supermarine company at Southampton Sir Robert acquired two things he considered of outstanding value: firstly, he got a stake in the flying boat business and an establishment by the water where they could be built and tested, for in those days of 1928 it looked very much as if the future of long-range commercial passenger and freight business lay with the flying boat; secondly, he acquired R.J. Mitchell, whose reputation as a designer was now sharply illuminated by the 1927 Schneider triumph and the great success of the Far East Flight by the Southampton flying boats.

It is no coincidence that the terms of the deal stipulated that Mitchell should remain with the company for at least five years.

R. J. Mitchell with Captain Wilkinson, responsible for developing the Napier Lion engine

CHAPTER 7

Turning to Rolls-Royce

After the 1927 Schneider race Mitchell had judged that the Napier Lion VIIB engine had, at 750 bhp, reached the practical limit of its power growth. So he decided to turn to Rolls-Royce to produce the substantially higher power now required for the next Schneider contest.

Conduit Street were hesitant about involving the company in a competitive and possibly risky venture of this nature and recommended Mitchell to discuss the matter with Sir Henry Royce himself, so Jimmy Bird and Mitchell visited that remarkable man in his house at West Wittering in West Sussex.

The story of Henry Royce is most unusual and merits a slight digression here. He was forty years old before, in his own words, he 'went in for cars'. Before he designed and made his first car in 1904 he had already built up, from very humble beginnings, a successful electrical engineering business in Manchester, F. H. Royce Ltd designing and building dynamos, generating plants and electrically powered cranes. He became interested, originally as a hobby or relaxation, in mechanically propelled vehicles and early motor cars and was unimpressed with what he considered their poor design. He decided to design and build a car himself and laid down three experimental models, the first of which emerged from the Cooke Street, Manchester, Works with Henry Royce himself at the wheel on 1 April 1904.

Royce was a natural and self-taught engineer. He was also an immensely hard worker who had known as a youth what it was to be grindingly poor. He had built up a successful business from virtually nothing with the help of a partner called Claremont who handled the financial and administrative side of the firm while Royce provided the drive, inspiration and meticulous engineering standards on the product side.

Royce believed that the internal combustion engine and its associated machinery — gearboxes, transmissions etc, could, if properly designed and engineered, be made to run silently and smoothly instead of with the racket and clatter kicked up by most of the motor-cars of that era. He also believed that only the highest engineering standards could achieve the reliability that he sought.

In 1904 he first met the Hon. C.S. Rolls, a young but experienced sporting motorist who had formed his own car sales and servicing company in London, C.S. Rolls & Co. Charles Rolls instantly recognized the quality of Royce's cars and so in 1906 came into being a company name, Rolls-Royce Limited, which was

Henry Royce in 1907, aged 44

The Roll-Royce Eagle engine of 1915. One of the most successful engines of the Great War, it powered the first direct Atlantic crossing, by a Vickers Vimy in 1919

The Vickers Vimy, flown by Alcock and Brown. It took off near St. John's, Newfoundland on 14th June, 1919 at the start of the first direct Atlantic flight of 1,890 miles. The successful flight ended at Clifden, Co. Galway 16 hr 27 min later although the Vimy was damaged through landing in boggy ground

destined for world-wide renown and to become an accepted symbol of quality and excellence in engineering.

In the new company Henry Royce dominated the design and engineering aspects while Claude Johnson and C.S. Rolls dominated what today we should call the marketing. By the outbreak of the First War in 1914 the Rolls-Royce car had well established its reputation as the best car in the world. Charles Rolls was killed in a flying accident in 1910, but not before he had seen to it that the Rolls-Royce car had become the natural conveyance of the aristocracy of England. By 1914 the company, under its wise and able General Managing Director Claude Johnson, had achieved a momentum which it has never lost.

The outbreak of war in 1914 closed off much of the luxury car market, but in fact production of the 40/50 hp chassis continued for use as armoured cars and staff cars until 1917.

In the meantime Henry Royce had turned his hand to the design of engines for aircraft. This involvement of Rolls-Royce in the design and production of aero-engines initially met with some opposition from the Board at Conduit Street, but as usual in such situations Royce had his way, aided by pressure from the War Office and the Admiralty.

So during the First War the company produced some highly

The Rolls-Royce 'R' type engine, developed from the Buzzard in less than six months. It gave 1900 hp for the Schneider Race in 1929, 2300 hp in 1931 and no less than 2530 hp for Stainforth's world speed record in September 1931

The 'R' type engine on the test-bed at Derby

Rod Banks, who developed the special fuels for the 1927, 1929 and 1931 Schneider Trophy contests as well as various world speed records, standing (in after years) beside the huge 24-cylinder Fiat AS.6 Tandem engine of 3000 hp which, installed in a Macchi MC72, took the world speed record for floatplanes at 440.681 mph on 23rd October 1934, a record which still stands.

Rod Banks helped to develop the fuel for this engine and also helped to solve some of the acute carburation problems

successful Royce-designed military engines — notably the Eagle* and the Falcon (designed by R. W. Harvey-Bailey).

By 1928 Royce had for some years been living and working remotely from the Works at Derby since the breakdown of his health due to the overwork and strain of the early years. As early as 1908 his fellow directors at Derby were discussing means of getting him away from the factory. Their desire was to persuade him to concentrate upon design, a field in which he had no equal, whereas there were others who could manage the factory and the administration of the company equally well.

This intent was not realized until 1911 when Royce suffered a major illness which nearly killed him. At this point Claude Johnson took the matter firmly in hand and established Royce at the Villa Mimosa at Le Canadel near St Tropez in the South of France (where Johnson also had a villa) during the winter, and at a house at St Margaret's Bay near Dover in summer, later moving to West Wittering in Sussex.

At these establishments there were always one or two resident designer/draughtsmen established in an annexe and A. G. Elliott (who became Chief Engineer after Royce's death in 1933), spent much time there and worked closely with Royce on both car and aero-engine design.

From these two retreats — at Le Canadel and West Wittering — Royce exercised close personal control over design at Derby. No major decision in the design and engineering fields could be taken without his approval and indeed he initiated most original projects himself. A design and engineering development organization had been built up at Derby over the years — with Ernest

---

*Two Rolls-Royce Eagles powered the first non-stop crossing of the North Atlantic by a Vickers Vimy in 1919.

The beautiful Gloster VI designed by H. P. Folland was plagued by problems with its highly super-charged Napier Lion en-gine and was withdrawn from the 1929 contest. The inverse-tapered wings were designed to improve control at low speeds

TOP LEFT: *Mitchell's S.6 of 1929*

LEFT: *S.6 'on the step', 1929*

Hives in charge of the experimental department and R.W. Harvey-Bailey as Chief Technical Production Engineer as key elements in it — which was well able to implement the ideas and wishes emanating from Henry Royce from the remoteness of his summer and winter retreats. Thus was a remarkable system of remote control established and made to work and the engineering genius of this extraordinary man was rescued and preserved to the immense benefit of the firm which he had originally created, and ultimately of the country.

It happened that in 1927 Royce had instructed Derby to prepare the design of a 60° V-Twelve engine of considerably greater cubic capacity than the Kestrel, which was the newest Rolls-Royce engine then in production for the Royal Air Force. This larger engine was called the Buzzard and was clearly designed to be capable of substantial future development and power growth. It passed its initial type tests in mid-1928, so that when Mitchell and Bird approached Royce at about that time on the subject of a new and much more powerful racing engine for the 1929 Schneider Trophy the basis for such an engine already existed. Royce agreed to go ahead but the company made no promises or guarantees of the power they expected to produce from the developed Buzzard engine. However, after a great deal of redesign and the addition of a large supercharger the 'R' type engine emerged from Derby in the incredibly short time of six months from go-ahead.

The high degree of supercharge was designed not to restore

TOP LEFT: *The elegant lines of H. P. Folland's Gloster – Napier VI, 1929*

RIGHT: *The 1929 British team*

CENTRE LEFT: *Macchi M.52 in steep turn, Calshot 1929*

RIGHT: *The 1929 Italian team*

LEFT: *Macchi M.67 at Calshot before the 1929 Schneider race. It was powered by a 1,800 hp Isotta-Frascini engine and flown by Lt. Remo Cadringher*

lost power at altitude (which hitherto had been the prime function of superchargers), but in order to run the engine at greatly increased manifold pressures, and thus BMEP (Brake Mean Effective Pressure), at sea-level.

Mitchell and his team at Supermarine designed the S.6 racing seaplane to take this 37-litre 'R' Type engine which for the 1929 race gave over 1,900 hp. The S.6 was a larger and technologically more advanced aircraft than the S.5 with, amongst other things, a more sophisticated cooling system.

At the same time Bill Folland of Gloster's produced the beauti-

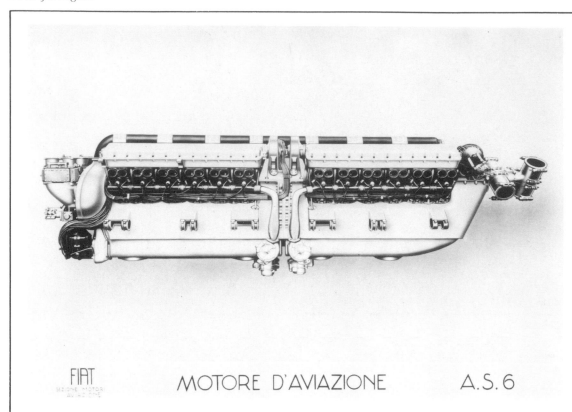

FIAT
SEZIONE MOTORI
AVIAZIONE

MOTORE D'AVIAZIONE   A.S.6

ful and elegant Gloster VI with the new supercharged Napier Lion engine of 1,320 hp. Unfortunately this aircraft was not able to race in 1929 because at the last minute it was bedevilled by fuel system problems, but it established a world speed record in 1929 of 336.3 mph, flown by George Stainforth.

The 1929 race was won at Calshot by Flying Officer H.R.D. Waghorn, RAF, in S.6 No N247 at 328.63 mph, with Dal Molin of Italy second in the Macchi M.52R at 285 mph.

After the 1929 race the Italians had also seen the need for great increases in available horse-power and Fiat embarked upon a revolutionary solution in which they coupled two of their light-weight AS.5 engines in tandem on a common crankcase driving two contra-rotating propellers, each engine driving its own propeller through two coaxial shafts.

The rearmost engine drove a centrifugal compressor used to supercharge both engines. This Fiat AS.6 engine of 50-litre cubic capacity eventually developed nearly 3,000 hp, but it encountered serious development problems after being installed in the Macchi Castoldi M.C.72, with the result that this very advanced aircraft never raced in a Schneider contest. However in 1933 and 1934 it twice beat the world speed record, raising it to 440.68 mph, a world's speed record for floatplanes, which still stands.

The Fiat AS.6 power unit of the Macchi MC72. This enormous engine was really two V-12 engines bolted end to end, each driving its own propeller, counter-rotating and using a common supercharger. The whole unit was 11 feet long, the induction pipe for 24 cylinders about 10 feet

CHAPTER 8

The 1931 race and World Speed Record

Preparations for the 1931 race were bedevilled by the decision of the British Government not to compete.

Admittedly the country was in the throes of an economic crisis, but it was a bad decision which caused great dismay amongst the aeronautical fraternity. Somewhat at the last moment the wealthy, public-spirited, and patriotic if eccentric Lady Houston offered £100,000 to cover the cost of British participation and sent a telegram to Ramsay Macdonald to that effect; the race was on again.

All this had caused a great and nearly fatal delay as far as designers and developers were concerned and the competitive threat from the Italian aircraft was very great — especially from the Macchi M.72 with the Fiat tandem engine. Rolls-Royce embarked urgently upon a programme to extract yet more power from the 'R' Type engine and Supermarine laid down two modified S.6s, to be called S.6B, capable of taking the more powerful engine. These aircraft had to be built in a tremendous hurry and it was due to the Herculean efforts of Trevor West-brook, the young, forceful and extremely energetic General

The Macchi MC72

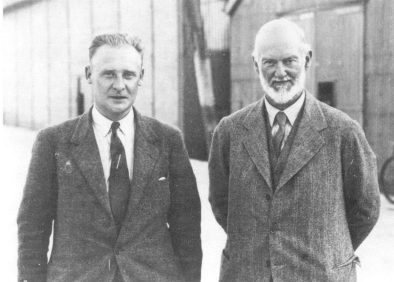

Manager of Supermarine, as well as of course of Mitchell's design team, that they were ready on time.

Throughout his career Mitchell showed an extraordinary capacity for making the right decision at the right moment, which is one of the most elusive characteristics necessary to a successful designer. A case in point was his decision that the Napier Lion VIIB of 1927 had reached the practical limit of its power growth, which led him to turn to a completely new engine from Rolls-Royce. Napiers had already decided to develop a supercharger for the Lion to give it a new lease of life and more power.

So in 1929 Mitchell had to choose between this and a new and untried engine from Rolls-Royce, who were not able to give any guarantees or firm indications of how much power it would produce. No one knows precisely what decided him to take the Rolls-Royce route — possibly it was his personal assessment of

The SB6B of 1931, S1596 powered by the Rolls-Royce 'R' type engine. The aircraft, flown by Flt Lieut George Stainforth, took the world speed record at 379.05 mph immediately after Bothman's victory in S1595 on 13 September 1931

Later, on 29 September, Stainforth, flying S1595, established a new absolute speed record of 407.5 mph with his 'R' type engine giving the remarkable power output of 2530 hp

such men as Sir Henry Royce, Elliott, Rowledge and Ernest Hives — but the decision turned out to be absolutely right, not only from the short-term point of view of winning the Schneider Trophy of 1929, but for the future longer-term collaboration between the two companies which became of such incalculable value to them and to Britain.

For 1931 the Italians had entered two MC.72 aircraft and the French a Bernard HV.220 and a Nieuport Delage. Sadly, neither team was ready in time for the race.

Therefore it became an unopposed fly-over for Great Britain, Flt. Lieut. John Boothman, RAF, completing the course in his S.6B at 340.08 mph with his 'R' Type engine giving 2,350 hp. Flt. Lieuts. Leonard Snaith and Frank Long stood by as reserves with the second S.6B and an S.6A. In spite of the lack of competitors huge crowds turned out to watch the fly-over. The aircraft was, after all, travelling at over half the speed of sound which in those days seemed both fantastic and exciting.

Shortly after the race Flt. Lieut. George Stainforth, RAF, gained the world speed record at 379.05 mph in Southampton Water in an S.6B S1596 which, two weeks later, he increased to 407.5 mph in S1595 with Rolls-Royce 'R' engine delivering the remarkable power output of 2,530 hp.

Here it is pertinent to remark that two years later (1933) Italy, having succeeded in solving its development problems with the MC.72 (which were in fact mostly engine problems), then set up a world speed record of 422.822 mph at Lake Garda and in 1934 they raised it again to 440.68 mph. The pilot for these records was Francesco Agello.

The British team in 1931. S1595, which took the world speed record on 29 September 1931, is on the extreme right. The two S.6Bs are on the outside, the S.6A (of 1929) in the centre

Thus were the Italians eventually rewarded for the great effort and enterprise they had put into the Schneider Trophy contests since 1926 during which period they had been Britain's main competitor.

This third successive victory for Britain in 1931 meant that the Schneider Trophy remained permanently in this country and so that famous contest, started by Jacques Schneider in 1913, was finished for ever.

Perhaps the series did not do much directly to fulfil Schneider's original intention, which was to stimulate the development of marine aircraft for commercial purposes, but there can be no doubt of the value to aviation in general arising from the rapid progress made in aerodynamic efficiency, structure, propellers, materials, hydrodynamics and the development of engines of high specific power, low specific weight, minimum frontal area and high reliability under conditions of extreme stress. All this was absorbed into the general sum of aeronautical knowledge in our country and it is hardly possible to identify any particular branch of aviation that did not in some way benefit.

Another fact which, certainly in retrospect, emerged from all this is that lessons learned in the course of such bursts of intense technological activity as the Schneider Trophy contests must, once properly absorbed, be put to immediate practical application otherwise they will be lost, as in Italy they were.

Dr. Ing. Ermanno Bazzocchi of Macchi, having discussed how the technologies gained from the Rolls-Royce 'R' Type engine of the S.6 and S.6B had given great impetus to the design of the Merlin engine which powered such famous and effective wartime aircraft as the Spitfire, Hurricane, Mustang, Lancaster and Mosquito, went on to say:

The victorious 1931 British Schneider team led by Orlebar

Sqn Ldr A. H. Orlebar DFC, the much respected Commander of the High Speed Flight in 1929 and 1931. He carried out the first flights and preliminary trials on both the S.6 and S.6B aircraft at Calshot

Unfortunately, it is sad to say, the same lesson was lost in Italy. Around 1933 the Italian Air Ministry decided to abandon the development of liquid-cooled engines for military use, and to concentrate on radial air-cooled power plants. So the costly and valuable experience of two decades of effort was wasted and when in 1940 the Italian industry again needed high-powered liquid-cooled engines, these had to be built under German licence.*

The Schneider Trophy contests, latterly at any rate, were in effect Government-sponsored full-scale research programmes conducted in an atmosphere of intense international competition. As far as Britain was concerned, our participation — so nearly cut off at a crucial moment by Ramsay Macdonald's Labour Government in 1930 — paid the most enormous and vital dividends, for had it not been for Supermarine's and Rolls-Royce's involvement in that struggle for technological supremacy it is very doubtful whether we should ever have seen the Spitfire or the Merlin and Griffon engines in the form in which they appeared in the country's most urgent hour of need.

If the speeds at which the Schneider Trophy was won between 1913 and 1931 are plotted we find that during the period of the contests the speed of the winning aircraft increased by a factor of about eight and the last world speed record set up by the Italian Macchi MC.72 was nearly ten times the speed of the race winner of 1913.

R.J. Mitchell, in one of the rare papers that he wrote on the subject (published in the Aeronautical Engineering Supplement to the *Aeroplane* of 25 December 1929) discussed in some detail the main problems associated with design of the Schneider seaplanes.

Some of Mitchell's general remarks are worthy of quotation these many years later. He wrote:

During the last ten years there has been an almost constant increase in the speed of our racing types. To maintain this steady increase very definite progress has been essential year by year. It has been necessary to increase the aerodynamic efficiency and the power-to-weight ratios of our machines, to reduce the consumption, and the frontal areas of our engines; to devise new methods of construction; and to develop the use of new materials. The results obtained in the form of speed have been a direct and absolute indication of our progress in aeronautical development . . . Speed in the air must always be a measure of aerodynamic efficiency which in turn must always be the most important consideration in all aircraft design.

Later in the same paper he wrote:

It is quite safe to say that the engine used in this year's winning S.6 machine in the Schneider Trophy contest would have taken

*Royal Aeronautical Society lecture.

ABOVE: A. G. Elliott ('E' in Rolls-Royce) who worked very closely with Henry Royce on the design of both Rolls-Royce cars and aero engines and became Chief Engineer of the company after Royce's death in 1933

ABOVE RIGHT: Cyril Lovesey. Great development engineer who worked on every Rolls-Royce engine from the Kestrel onwards, and whose contribution to the success of the Merlin was enormous.

As Hooker's work on superchargers had the effect of doubling the power of the Merlin during the war years Lovesey's job was to maintain the reliability and mechanical integrity of the engine – a difficult job magnificently done

at least three times as long to produce under normal processes of development had it not been for the spur of international competition. There is little doubt that this intensive engine development will have a very profound effect on our aircraft during the next few years.

These words were written at the end of 1929, some three years before. Hitler came to power in Germany. Mitchell could not then have known just how profound an effect the latter-day Schneider contests were to have — and how soon.

Cyril Lovesey was a most distinguished and senior development engineer at Rolls-Royce who was engaged in the development of all Rolls-Royce piston engines from the Kestrel onwards, including the 'R' Type Schneider engine, and then played a major and vital role in the development of the Merlin. He summed up the main areas in which experience with the 'R' Type engine provided important lessons which were fully exploited in the Second World War.

These he itemized as follows:

a) Fuels
b) Valve cooling
c) Supercharging
d) Mechanical developments to take care of the high output made possible by fuels and supercharging

That sums it up, in the few words typical of Cyril Lovesey, but covering a vast area of meaning.

CHAPTER 9

The F.7/30 Fighter

During 1930, and thus well before the outcome of the 1931 Schneider contest was known, the Air Ministry started work on a specification for a new single-seat fighter aircraft basically intended as a replacement for the Bristol Bulldog with which most of the Squadrons of the Fighting Area of ADGB (Air Defence of Great Britain — the predecessor of Fighter Command) were equipped.

In fact this specification was not issued for competitive tender to industry until October 1931, but it still retained its prefix F.7/30. The reason for the delay in issuing this specification was almost certainly that the technical branches of the Air Ministry estimated that an engine of around 700hp would be needed to meet the specification, and that in 1930 no suitable service engine of this power existed. By October 1931, however, Rolls-Royce had satisfactorily type tested the 21.24 litre Goshawk engine of 660bhp (which embodied steam, or evaporative, cooling), and the Air Ministry no doubt then felt that in issuing the F.7/30 specification they were not asking industry for the impossible.

At that time the significant background situation was that we had in Britain an aircraft design team at Supermarine who were world leaders in the technology of high-speed aircraft, and an engine design team at Rolls-Royce who had brought the 60° V-Twelve supercharged engine of high specific power, low specific weight and low frontal area to a new pitch of efficiency and performance.

The logic of this situation demanded that these two teams should now collaborate in the design of a fighter, and the F.7/30 specification emerged at precisely the right moment to enable them to do so.

The F.7/30 specification (see Appendix) required the highest possible speed at 15,000 feet, the highest possible rate of climb, good manoeuvrability, four .303 machine-guns, all-metal construction and good fighting view for the pilot; all this to be combined with a landing speed not exceeding 60 mph. Either a monoplane or a biplane was acceptable, as was any type of British engine.

In 1931 industry in Britain was still suffering from the effects of world recession, and the issue of the F.7/30 specification sparked off intense competition among the aircraft companies. Three monoplane and two biplane designs were submitted.

Mitchell's design was designated the Supermarine Type 224 and embodied the new Rolls-Royce Goshawk engine with evaporative cooling. This latter was an attempt to solve the then

The Supermarine F.7/30 fighter, powered with Rolls-Royce evaporatively cooled Goshawk engine

rapidly increasing problem of cooling drag by running the engine at temperatures above boiling-point, passing the steam emerging from the cylinder jackets through surface condensers situated in the wing leading edges, returning the condensate to a collector sump and recirculating it through the engine. In effect this system was exploiting the latent heat of the vaporization of water.

The Type 224, with a cranked monoplane wing, a fixed trousered undercarriage and an open cockpit made its first flight, at Eastleigh in the hands of Mutt Summers, Vickers' Chief Test Pilot, in February 1934.

The aeroplane was not a success; the top speed was disappointing, the rate of climb was below specification requirement, the steam cooling system was far from being satisfactorily developed, the aircraft was overweight and the drag patently too high.

Thus, although the Schneider Trophy had been dominated by monoplane designs since 1926, the problems of adapting the monoplane to the broader, more stringent and comprehensive requirements of an operational fighter aircraft were not yet solved. The F.7/30 competition was eventually won by a biplane design from Glosters which went in to RAF service in 1937 as the Gladiator. By mid-1934 Mitchell had already started work on a radically revised version of his Type 224 design.

Mitchell worked on his revised design against a steadily worsening international situation in Europe. In May 1933 the Foreign Office in London had warned the Government that the Germany of Adolf Hitler was re-arming, particularly in the air. Then in October 1933 tension mounted as Germany withdrew from the Disarmament Conference in Geneva and left the League of Nations.

Still fresh in every Englishman's mind at this time were the chilling words uttered by Stanley Baldwin to Parliament in 1932: 'The bomber will always get through.' For a while Britain continued her efforts at Geneva to exercise some control over air re-armament, but all to no avail. On 28 June 1934 the Geneva talks collapsed.

In the wake of Germany's departure from Geneva the British Government initiated a comprehensive survey of the worst deficiencies of the nation's defences, and agreement was quickly reached that priority must be given to air defence. Within days of the collapse of the Geneva talks the Air Ministry was able to present the Cabinet with an expansion scheme for the Royal Air Force known as Scheme 'A'. This called for an additional 41 squadrons to be formed and equipped by 31 March 1939 and was approved by the Government and announced to Parliament on 19 July 1934.

Seven days later, on 26 July, Mitchell's redesign of the Type 224 was submitted to the Air Ministry in Supermarine specification No.425a.

Mitchell's new proposal eliminated the anhedral centre section reducing the span to 39ft 4in, and the trousered landing gear was replaced by a retractable undercarriage. The evaporative-cooled Goshawk engine was retained, the wing was still straight tapered and the armament four .303 machine-guns, two in the fuselage and two in the wings. The estimated all-up weight was 4,700lb.

In the meantime Rolls-Royce had been working since early 1933 on the design of a new supercharged V-Twelve engine of 27-litre capacity with a target power output of 1,000 hp (See Chapter 10).

In the same month that Scheme 'A' was announced — July 1934 — a development model of this new engine, temporarily known as the PV-12 but destined for undying fame as the Merlin, successfully completed its first 100-hour type test. At this stage the engine was rated at only 790 hp, but results so far encouraged Rolls-Royce — and others — in the belief that the magic figure of 1,000 hp was in sight.

Mitchell was quick to appreciate the potential of the new engine and the prospect it offered of a great increase in the performance of his new fighter — and by December 1934 the decision was made to embody it in the revised Type 224.

It was too soon for there to be any Air Ministry finance behind either Mitchell's new aircraft design or Rolls-Royce's new PV-12 engine. Both therefore were supported by company money — indeed the PV prefix to the new engine stood for Private Venture — and in November 1934 the Board of Vickers Ltd voted the sum of £10,000 to enable Mitchell and his team to continue with the design of the Type 300, as it was now designated. Thus at this stage both aircraft and engine were proceeding on a Private Venture or company-funded basis.

Sir Robert McLean, the Chairman of Vickers (Aviation) Ltd (sole owners of the Supermarine Aviation Works), believed that the failure of the Type 224 aircraft had been largely due to the restrictive nature of the F.7/30 Air Ministry specification.

There was something in this theory in so far that the requirement for such a low landing speed probably led to too large a wing, but it was probably dubious to blame the whole thing on the terms of specification.

Nonetheless Sir Robert felt strongly about it and wrote to the Air Ministry informing them that Mitchell's new design was proceeding at the company's expense and that no official interference with the design would be tolerated. At the same time he had informed Mr Sidgreaves, Managing Director of Rolls-Royce, that Vickers were proceeding with the design of 'a new killer fighter' and that he had given instructions to Mitchell that no official interference with the design was to be accepted.

However, Mitchell was too old and experienced a hand to believe that his design could proceed totally without consultation with and co-operation from the Air Staff, the technical branches of the Air Ministry or the Research Establishments. Whilst he undoubtedly valued the freedom of action which Sir Robert's somewhat radical pronouncements had afforded him he proceeded according to his own judgement, steering a wise and careful course, and relations with the Air Staff and with Farnborough continued to run smoothly. The situation was neatly summed up by J.D. Scott in his *Vickers, a History*; referring to Sir Robert's instruction he wrote:

> This was the pure milk of the private-venture gospel, and in the historical form that Sir Robert McLean gave to it, it certainly expresses the intentions he had at the time of the initiation of the design. But the design of an aircraft is a large venture, in which, in one way and another, many people are involved. By the 1930s, and indeed much earlier, these people — in the firms, in the Air Ministry, at Farnborough and Martlesham Heath — had formed habits and friendships. It was not easy to break these habits and friendships by an administrative fiat.
>
> This was particularly so with Mitchell in 1934 and 1935, for he was leading a threatened life; he had already had an operation for cancer and while he hoped that this had been completely successful, he looked coolly at the alternative. If time were to be short he would need the best advice.
>
> So there was in the design of the new aircraft more co-operation than was officially envisaged; particularly at Wing Commander level with the Air Ministry in London and on purely technical matters with the RAE.

So Supermarine design work on the revised Type 224 proceeded during 1934 and notwithstanding Sir Robert McLean's attitude the Air Staff took a lively interest in it, especially Air Marshal Sir Hugh Dowding, the member of the Air Council for Research and Development (AMRD). In December 1934 he placed a contract with Supermarine for a single prototype aircraft.

Thus the period of private venture design of the revised 224 (Type 300) was short-lived, but its importance in the evolution of Mitchell's design which eventually became the Spitfire must not be underestimated.

CHAPTER 10

Ernest Hives and the Merlin Engine

(by Alec Harvey-Bailey)

To the generation involved in aviation before and during the Second World War the name Merlin is synonymous with Rolls-Royce and represents a peak in aero-engine development. While many contributed to Merlin's success, two names formed the driving force to this end. The first was Sir Henry Royce and the second E.W. Hives, later Lord Hives, known universally by his Rolls-Royce reference 'Hs'. The lineage of the Merlin can be traced from Sir Henry's first aero engine, the Eagle of 1915, through his later designs to the 'R' Type Schneider Trophy engine, which set new standards for power development. It was from the achievements of the 'R' Type that Royce and Hives saw that a world-beating military engine could be produced, developing greater specific powers than had previously been thought possible.

From the Eagle came the 60° V-Twelve, liquid-cooled, single overhead cam concept. The later and larger capacity Condor espoused the 4-valve head and single spur reduction gear. Putting these together in the 'F' or Kestrel Royce added the new generation of aluminium alloys, the lightweight wet linered cylinder block and the supercharger. It was the success of the Kestrel that created the idea of Rolls-Royce's being asked to design a racing engine. The Napier-powered Supermarine S5 had won the 1927 Schneider Trophy race at Venice by a narrow margin and a much greater turn of speed would be required to defeat the brilliant and determined Italians in the next contest in 1929 at Calshot in England.

Late in 1927 Royce instructed Derby to design an engine similar to the Kestrel, but having a somewhat larger bore and stroke of 6 × 6.6 in. Significantly he instructed that each cylinder should have two extra holding-down studs, known as saddle studs. The new engine, the 'H' or Buzzard, passed a type test in June 1928 and Royce sent a telegram to Derby on 13 June: 'Wormald, Bailey Roycar Derby. Extremely pleased with excellent work done introducing larger aero engine so quickly thanks to your efforts and those assisting. Royce.' Although a decision was not taken to proceed with a racing engine until February 1929 it is evident that Royce had seen in the 'H' engine the basis of a heavily super-charged racing powerplant and it was for this reason that he instructed the extra cylinder holding-down studs.

From 1916 Ernest Hives had been Head of the Experimental Department and had worked with Royce on aero and chassis development, showing not only technical ability but the drive to

NEAR RIGHT: *Ernest Hives ('Hs'). The man who led and guided Rolls-Royce through the design and development of the Merlin and through the 1939–45 war. Not only did he preside over the out-standing development effort on the Merlin and Griffon engines, but also over the massive production effort in both Britain and the United States. He also led Rolls-Royce into the jet age.*

In recognition of his great contribution to the British war effort he was created the first Baron Hives in 1950.

'The inspiration behind the entire Merlin programme, following the death of Sir Henry Royce, was Hs, later Lord Hives. He wrought his success with his team of often turbulent barons and an army of workers'

ABOVE RIGHT: *Stanley (later Sir Stanley) Hooker. Sir Kenneth Keith – Chairman of Rolls-Royce 1972– 1980 described him as 'this brilliant mathematician, who won almost every available scholarship and academic prize'.*

He joined Rolls-Royce in January 1938 at Derby. Fluid dynamics was his basic subject and he quickly immersed himself in increasing the efficiency of the supercharger for the Merlin engine, which was already flying in the Hurricane and the Spitfire

Hooker shared an office with Cyril Lovesey and this 'duo', working together, were very largely responsible for the spectacular power growth of the Merlin during the war

get things done on time, a quality sometimes lacking in engineers and designers. With only six months to go, the race being on the first weekend in September, Hives took charge of the development programme, converting the designs of Royce and his staff into hardware. To produce the 'R' from the 'H' required a big new supercharger with double-sided impeller, new cylinder blocks with angled sparking plug holes and rocker covers that formed part of the cowling line to reduce drag and improve cooling. The task was to achieve 1,500 hp at a weight of 1 lb per hp and on the first run 1,545 hp at 2,750 rpm was recorded. By the time of the race the engine had an endurance capability of 1,900 hp at 3,000 rpm, sufficient to demonstrate a convincing win for R.J. Mitchell's S.6. It is history that due to vacillation by the Government only a few months were available to produce a more powerful engine for the 1931 race. To achieve a reliable 2,350 hp and 2,530 hp for a subsequent world record flight much redesign was entailed. This included a new crank with integral balance weights, a master and articulated rod assembly in place of a fork and blade rod, new valve springs and sodium-cooled exhaust valves. Although the race was a fly-over the superiority of Mitchell's S.6B and Royce's modified 'R' engine were clearly demonstrated. Rolls-Royce had gained prestige and Hives had emerged as the outstanding experimental engineer in Britain and probably the world.

After these events Hives saw that a blend of Kestrel reliability and 'R' performance was an achievable target and in all probability convinced Royce without too much difficulty. The result was that before he died in the spring of 1933 Royce had laid down the

key attributes of a new engine, started as a private venture and thus named PV12. It is significant that with the success of the 'R' before him Royce chose a bore and stroke of 5.4 × 6 in. instead of using the larger cylinder of the racing engine. He evidently recognized then that the smaller bore would produce a more reliable cylinder assembly, with better combustion, thus lending itself to high boost developments on aviation petrol as opposed to a racing blend.

The design was completed and the engine was first run in the autumn of 1933 when it gave 625 hp. Development continued, 790 hp being reached, and in the spring of 1935 it flew in a modified Hart. The design contained two new features: the cylinder blocks and crankcase were in one piece, with detachable cylinder heads, and there was a double helical reduction gear, both of which gave trouble. Elliott, who had succeeded Royce as Chief Engineer, undertook a redesign reverting to a spur gear and detachable cylinder blocks. Single-cylinder research had shown apparent advantages in a ramp head and the new design included this feature in a two-piece cylinder block. On main engine test it did not give the anticipated power and was subject to cracking, but the Merlin, as it was now called, was close to its target of 1,000 hp. This configuration of engine powered the first Spitfire, which flew early in 1936. Hives appreciated that the problems with the cylinders had no quick solution. He decided to revert to a single-piece cylinder block, similar in principle to that used on the Kestrel, while the design of a two-piece block with a single plane cylinder head was started.

The years following Royce's death were difficult for the company. There was no dominant personality in the lead. Wormald, the General Works Manager and Director, was in failing health and he died before the end of 1936. The Board then appointed Hives to this position, making him a Director a few months later.

It was a popular appointment with the senior executives at Derby who responded to his leadership. Now he was not only faced with the experimental tasks of aero and chassis, but with the management and reorganization of the Derby factory, to improve its efficiency and prepare for a war with Germany, which he saw to be inevitable. By this time the single-piece block Merlin was performing well and in June 1937 a Merlin II, the definitive production engine, completed 100 hours' flying in a Horsley in 6½ days. Towards the end of the year a satisfactory Air Ministry type test was completed.

Throughout 1937 Hives' reorganization continued. In July separate Aero and Chassis Divisions were created, A.G. Elliott becoming Chief Engineer — Aero Division, and R.W. Harvey-Bailey, who had been Chief Technical Production Engineer, became Chief Engineer, Chassis Division. To provide an input of young engineers to complement his old guard an engineering apprenticeship scheme was started and a number of engineering pupils were engaged to be forerunners of the graduate apprentices.

Having refurbished the Derby Works, expansion to meet the re-armament programme was a pressing necessity, although it was almost impossible to get firm programmes from Air Ministry. At the beginning of 1938 orders for the Merlin were cut from 2,220 to 1,470. The shadow scheme, which enabled established Bristol engines to be produced by the motor industry, did not appeal to Hives. He realized the great potential of the Merlin and wished to have control of its destiny so that improved engines could be progressively introduced with the minimum disruption to output. He was sufficiently persuasive with the Air Ministry on this issue so that when the Crewe factory was started in June 1938 as a 'shadow' to Derby, it was accepted that it would be treated as an extension of Rolls-Royce. At the time of Munich he was able to report that 1,700 Merlins had been delivered and by June 1939 the first Crewe-built engine had been put to test. Coincidentally with this the company were asked to build another factory at Glasgow to make Merlins, to be managed under contract to Air Ministry.

Production of single-speed, single-stage, supercharged Merlins which would carry the brunt of the air fighting in 1940 was now in full swing. The important thing was to have a follow-up of more powerful engines. Among Hives's young intake were Stanley (later Sir Stanley) Hooker and Geoff Wilde, who rapidly became specialists in supercharger development, leading to the central entry blower and the big two-stage supercharger and intercooler that were to transform Merlin power and altitude performance.

When war broke out Hives was able to call on a strong technical team at Derby which included Elliott, Ellor, Lovesey, Rubbra, Dorey, Hall and Harvey-Bailey, whom he recalled from the Chassis Division. Although production was of the utmost importance Hives was always looking for better engines. The air fighting in 1940 was largely supported by Merlin IIs and IIIs, giving 1,030 hp at 16,000 ft, and taking advantage of 100 octane fuel at lower altitudes to run at 12lb boost. A number of Merlin XIIs with

geared-up superchargers saw service in the Battle of Britain, giving more power at altitude. Due to Hives's pressure the Merlin 45 and 46 were available at the beginning of 1941, with full throttle heights of around 20,000 ft and some 12% more power for the Spitfire V. While this was going on decisions had been taken for the Ford Motor Company to set up a Merlin factory at Trafford Park and in Detroit the Packard Motor Company had taken on a similar task.

The fighter air war was showing the need for still more powerful Merlins and on Christmas Day 1941 the first Merlin 61 was dispatched. This engine, with the two-stage supercharger and two-piece cylinder blocks, was to transform Spitfire performance, being followed in 1943 by the Merlin 66 giving over 1,600 hp at 16,000 ft using 3,000 rpm + 18lb boost, the limit possible on 100 octane fuel. The advent of 150 grade fuel allowing 25lb boost put over 2,000 hp into the pilot's throttle hand with no loss of reliability. In parallel with the Merlin Hives had had a team working on the Griffon, an engine of 6 in. bore × 6.6 in. stroke, the same size as the 'R' Type. Early in 1943 Griffon VI-powered Spitfire XIIs were in service with the Home Defence squadrons of Fighter Command to counter the low-level Fw190 fighter bombers, and by January 1944 two-stage supercharged Griffons were in service in Spitfire XIVs giving 1,800 hp at 21,000 ft and 2,375 hp at 25lb boost low level. Thus a range of Merlins and Griffons was available to provide optimum power for the various Marks of

An early Merlin flying test-bed, the Hawker Horsley at Hucknall

Spitfire from sea level to well over 40,000 ft for high-altitude interception and photographic reconnaissance. Sample Merlin-powered Spitfire IXs were regularly test-flown to 46,000 ft

In 1943 Hives was made a Companion of Honour in recognition of his unswerving efforts to produce more and better engines. He never lost sight of the sacrifices made by RAF aircrew and listened intently to reports from his liaison pilots who had open access to squadron pilots. A typical example of his tenacity and drive is shown in his dealings with Lord Beaverbrook, then Minister of Aircraft Production, in the autumn of 1940. Hives had found that there was a view in MAP that the Sabre was the coming fighter engine and resources were being diverted to it at the expense of the Merlin. He was pressing for more powerful Merlins for fighters and in a letter to Beaverbrook said: 'We know the position as regards fighter aircraft and it is *positively certain* that the only machines we shall have to fight the Germans in 1941 are the Hurricanes and Spitfires . . . When we see an aircraft programme which calls for Merlin IIIs up to the end of 1941, we say we are just not trying. If it is laid down that commencing early next year all the Hurricanes and Spitfires must be fitted with Merlin XX engines [the Merlin 45/46 issue still unsettled] Rolls-Royce have got the most difficult part of the programme, *but we have got to do it, and we can do it.*' It was in this vein that he led Rolls-Royce throughout the war. When peace came he tackled the post-war reconstruction with his usual vision and vigour.

In January 1946 Hives was appointed Managing Director of the company. In 1950 his wartime efforts were truly recognized, in particular his management of the total Merlin programme, and he was raised to the peerage with a barony. On 31 October he was made Chairman of the Board, continuing to lead the company until he retired at the age of seventy in January 1957. He died in 1965, remembered by many as the man who did more for Rolls-Royce than anyone but Sir Henry Royce himself. Those who had worked for him could feel in the words of Shakespeare that they had experienced 'a little touch of Harry in the night'.

CHAPTER 11

The Design Evolves

At this stage Mitchell's revised Type 224 design was regarded by AMRD (Dowding) as a second bite at the F.7/30 cherry, and Mitchell was proposing physically to modify the existing prototype Type 224 and to incorporate the new Rolls-Royce PV-12 engine in place of the Goshawk. But in the meantime the operational requirements branch of the Air Ministry were working on a new specification to supersede the F.7/30, with considerably augmented performance requirements and greater lethality of armament, which was eventually to emerge as the F.10/35, which called for a minimum of six, and preferably eight, guns.

It is clear from surviving documents relating to suggestions coming up from within the Services (which had been encouraged by the Air Ministry) that the concept of multi-gun fighters was already gaining acceptance as early as February or March 1933. In particular a Wing Commander A. T. Williams, who died in June 1934, seems to have been an early proponent of the concept so that by 1934 it was not an entirely novel idea.

Squadron Leader Ralph Sorley, of the Operational Requirements Branch at the Air Ministry, had with the collaboration of Major Thomson of the Directorate of Armament Development established by actual tests carried out at Shoeburyness that for a fighter to inflict lethal damage to an all-metal bomber it would be necessary to achieve not fewer than 256 strikes with .303 ammunition. At the same time it was the judgement of the Air Staff that a fighter attacking a bomber flying at 180 mph would be most unlikely to achieve more than a two-second firing burst. Simple arithmetic therefore showed that with a firing rate of approximately 1,000 rounds per minute per gun at least eight guns would be needed to achieve the desired lethality in two seconds.

So eight guns became the policy for RAF fighters and Sorley had it written into what was to become the F.10/35 specification. It was however a considerable departure from established practice in so far as that the guns had to be mounted in the wings firing outside the propeller disc. This meant that the guns were well outside the line of sight, involving harmonization problems, and there would be no way of clearing stoppages in the air. Against this the advantages were great in that interrupter gear was eliminated and a lethal rate of fire achieved.

In the meantime Sorley discovered that AMRD (Dowding) had placed orders for a single prototype of a new design by Sydney Camm of Hawkers, and for a single prototype of Mitchell's revised Type 224 design, both of which had the four guns which had been called for in the old F.7/30 specification.

Dowding had regarded these two prototypes as largely experimental types which merited official support, but it quickly became clear to Sorley that both types went a long way towards meeting the new F.10/35 specification, still in draft and not yet issued. Sorley went to see both Camm and Mitchell — and this was after the two prototypes had been ordered — and persuaded them to incorporate eight guns instead of four in their prototypes. A special specification, F.37/34, had been issued to cover the building of the experimental prototype to the revised Type 300 design which Dowding had ordered from Supermarine.

It is interesting to note that the F.37/34 specification is headed 'Experimental High Speed Single Seat Fighter'. It was issued on 3 January 1935, was couched in fairly broad terms and made frequent reference to the F.7/30 specification. Paragraph 3 opens as follows:

3. *Load to be Carried*
The Service load shall be as defined in F.7/30 except for departures which may subsequently be agreed between the contractor and the Director of Technical Development . . .

It would have been under this very flexible clause that the armament requirement was increased from four to eight guns by negotiation during 1935.

Other important changes to the design were incorporated during 1935, apart from the armament.

The first was to the cooling system. The steam cooling of the Goshawk in the F.7/30 had never been wholly satisfactory so early revised 224 designs embodied what was known as compositive cooling. This was in effect evaporative cooling using wing condensers, but with provision for a small auxiliary radiator recessed into the structure which would be extended for take-off and climb but effectively retracted for high-speed flight. Mitchell provided a recess for this auxiliary radiator within the structure of the starboard wing.

Then, as a result of a visit to the United States by Cyril Lovesey, Rolls-Royce decided to go for ethylene glycol cooling which appeared to be more efficient and which greatly reduced the

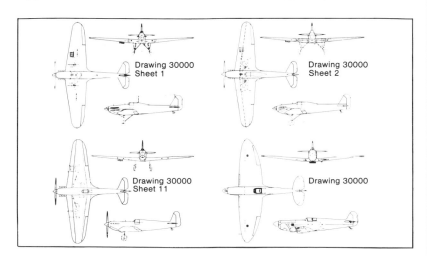

Supermarine Spec. No. 425 – Successive refinements

volume of coolant required and enabled a much smaller radiator to be used. More or less concurrently with all this Dr Frederick Meredith of the Royal Aircraft Establishment at Farnborough developed the ducted radiator system in which, by enclosing the radiator in a convergent/divergent duct, the assembly could be half buried in the structure, the intake area greatly reduced and the discharge air accelerated to produce a propulsive effect, thereby reducing the overall drag of the installation. And so it happened that the radiator for the new glycol cooling, much smaller than it would have been for pure water cooling, and ducted in accordance with Dr Meredith's proposals, fitted neatly in the structural recess originally planned for the compositive cooling system in the starboard wing, the oil cooler being placed within a duct under the port wing.

The second important change was from a straight taper of the wing plan form to the famous and elegant elliptical wing shape which was to become the Spitfire's most distinctive visual feature.

An aspect of the wing design which Mitchell was most determined upon was the achievement of a thin wing section, defined as a wing of low thickness/chord ratio. In fact he achieved a wing of 13% T/C ratio at the root reducing to 6% at the tip. This was only made possible by the use of very advanced and sophisticated structural design of the wing which was, of course, an entirely cantilever structure. The high predicted performance of the aircraft required very great strength and stiffness.

So when Ralph Sorley came along and wanted two more guns added to each wing it presented a considerable problem for Mitchell, whose wing was very much thinner than Camm's wing on the Hurricane. Mitchell was determined not to ease up on his thickness/chord requirements and his staff pointed out that with an elliptical plan form a greater chord and hence a greater actual thickness could be maintained further out along the wing span than with a straight tapered wing. This would give just enough room to install two more guns each side outboard of the original four-gun installation.

An elliptical wing also had certain attractions to the aerodynamicists in reduced drag under level flight conditions at altitude. This explanation of the matter is appropriate because it has been fairly widely suggested that the Spitfire's elliptical wing was copied from the Heinkel HE 70 which was imported from Germany in 1936 to act as a flying test-bed at Rolls-Royce, Hucknall. While the Supermarine design department undoubtedly studied carefully some of the excellent features of this aircraft, the elliptical wing shape was not one of the features they copied; in fact the wing of the S.4 (some ten years earlier) had been elliptical in plan.

The close involvement of the Air Staff leading to the eight-gun installation, itself leading to the change in the plan form of the wing, and the close involvement of the Royal Aircraft Establishment at Farnborough, especially in the matter of the ducted radiator system for both Hurricane and Spitfire, tends to illustrate Mitchell's wisdom in deciding that his design could not proceed in isolation from the Air Staff and the technical Establishments.

CHAPTER 12

Scapas, Stranraers and A.G. Pickering

During all the activity with the Schneider races from 1927 to 1931 a great deal of flying-boat work, Supermarine's main stock-in-trade, had also been in progress.

Some three-engined layouts, based largely on the old Southampton hull form, had been built and tested but these had produced disappointing performance results and had not gone into production.

Finally a completely new design of boat with three engines known as the Southampton Mk. X was designed and built as a replacement for the successful and well-tried Southampton II in the RAF's Maritime Reconnaissance Squadrons.

This project was started in 1929 and by this time Supermarine had been taken over by Vickers (Aviation) Ltd at Weybridge. The new hull was built at the Woolston Works and the new wings and superstructure including engine mountings were built at Weybridge. Both came out fairly considerably over their design weight with the result that the flight performance of the Southampton X was very much below specification requirements. The prototype first flew, with Mutt Summers at the controls, in March 1930 with three Armstrong Siddeley Jaguar VIC engines. In endeavours to improve its poor performance these were subsequently changed to Armstrong Siddeley Panthers, and yet a later change to Bristol XFBMs was made. Various attempts were also made to lighten the structure, but neither the increases in power nor the marginal savings in weight were sufficient to restore the shortfall in specification performance.

The Southampton Mk. X (and about the only connection with the original Southampton was in the perpetuation of the name) must therefore be counted amongst Supermarine's failures, and it had much to do with the firm's later abandonment of the three-engined formula and its return to the twin-engined layout so successfully used later with the Scapa and the Stranraer.

However, one more three-engined boat was to be designed and built before the formula was finally abandoned. This was a project of radically different design in that it was a parasol monoplane with a decidedly slab-sided hull design, angular 'sawn-off' configuration to both mainplane and tailplane and sponsons protruding from the lower hull to provide stability on the water in place of wing-tip floats.

The design of the Air Yacht, as it was called, was somewhat redolent of some of the contemporary Dornier flying boat designs in Germany and the use of sponsons for water stability was in line with both the American and German practice of the time.

The concept of an Air Yacht had its early origins in one of Supermarine's previous excursions into the three-engined layout, which was virtually a Southampton Mk II with three Armstrong Siddeley Jaguar IIIA engines built in 1927 to the order of the Royal Danish Navy, as a torpedo launcher, and to be called the Nanok.

It narrowly failed to meet its specification performance and the RDN declined to accept it, leaving it on Supermarine's hands. This was in 1927 and Supermarine refitted the hull internally to what we should today call a VIP or luxury executive standard and sold the aircraft to the Hon. A.E. Guinness as a private air yacht. It received the civil registration G-AAAB, and was renamed the Solent.

Guinness used it regularly for flights from Hythe on Southampton water and to Dun Laoghaire harbour, Dublin, and thence on to Lough Corrib near his home in Galway. The Solent had luxurious accommodation for both owner and guests.

Then, in 1930, appeared the aforementioned slab-sided three-engined monoplane design called the Air Yacht and built to the order of A.E. Guinness as a replacement for his Solent.

Whilst the concept perhaps had its origins in the successful Solent, the actual air yacht as it emerged in 1930 represented a complete departure from previous Supermarine design practice. Again there was a shortfall in performance and the original Armstrong Siddeley Jaguars were replaced by Panthers and a certificate of airworthiness was granted on 22 December 1931 after trials at the MAEE Felixstowe.

However, A.E. Guinness declined to accept the Air Yacht on the grounds that it failed to meet its specification and once again Supermarine were left with a redundant and expensive aircraft on their hands. Once more, however, a wealthy and somewhat eccentric lady came to the rescue in the shape of Mrs June James, who saw it by chance and bought it from Supermarine with the intention of using it for cruising in the Mediterranean.

She also took on Henri Biard, on a secondment basis from Supermarine, as her pilot.

Mrs James was a woman not only of great wealth, enormous determination and courage, but also a total lack of any sort of knowledge or understanding of the practicalities of aviation. This was obviously a potentially explosive combination.

In the words of C.F. Andrews and E.B. Morgan,* 'eventually on 11 October 1932 the Air Yacht (with Henri Biard at the controls) sailed off down Southampton Water into the wide blue yonder to adventures that defy description'.

Tommy Rose eventually joined the party as another pilot and those of us who knew dear old Tommy as well as Henri Biard can fully understand that the situation would indeed very soon have defied description! Eventually the Air Yacht was impounded by the authorities at Capri against a salvage claim and the only parts

Supermarine Aircraft since 1914, C.F. Andrews and E.B. Morgan (Putnam)

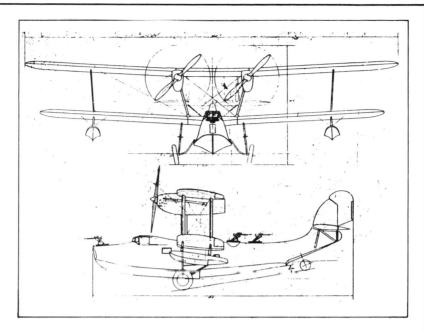

Scapa on beaching trolley

eventually to find their way back to England were the engines.

After these somewhat disastrous excursions into the three-engined flying-boat formula Supermarine designed a boat as a replacement for the Southampton II using two Rolls-Royce Kestrel engines and based very largely on the old Southampton hull form, but with much cleaner and less draggy superstructure and engine installations.

The following is an extract from a report by Arthur Shirval, one of Mitchell's senior designers who specialized in hull forms:

A change of policy in 1931 favouring twin-engined flying boats in place of the somewhat unsuccessful three-engined boats recently produced, rendered it obvious that our best course was to revert to the Southampton Mk. II — a type that had proved itself during years of service in the RAF to be a really sound and reliable job with good general performance — and use it for the development of a new design.

With reference to the hull of the aircraft, this course had been strongly urged five years previously but a policy of economy with a resultant tendency towards rectangular sections, flat plates and square corners had caused the proposal to be disregarded.

Since no tank testing was conducted on models of the Mk. II until after the machine was built the success of the hull must be attributed to pure chance.

Compared with its predecessors and certain also of its successors its lines were good and it is generally recognized in marine work that a pretty boat is likely to be a good boat . . . The performance of this hull (Southampton Mk. II), as demonstrated subsequently full-scale and also in the tank, was sufficiently remarkable to justify its use as the basis on which to shape a new improved form.*

Thus the new Kestrel-engined boat to A.M. Specification R.20/31 initially called the Southampton IV had a hull based essentially upon the lines of the old and well-tried Southampton, but with much improved topsides embodying enclosed cockpits for the pilots and improved accommodation for the crew and the detail design updated in line with current technology.

Mutt Summers made the first flight in the Southampton IV at Woolston on 8 July 1932 and carried out the subsequent contractor's trials before it was collected on 29 October by MAEE Felixstowe in the person of Flt. Lieut. Ardly George Pickering, then one of the MAEE test pilots.

This was the beginning of a long and fruitful association between Supermarine and George Pickering, which was to last through the remainder of his service in the RAF at Felixstowe and his subsequent employment as a test pilot at Supermarine until his death.

Type approval was given to the Southampton IV at Felixstowe in April 1933 and a month later George Pickering took it to Kalafrana in Malta on attachment to No. 202 Flying Boat Squadron for extended service trials which included proving flights to Gibraltar and back and a cruise to Port Sudan via Sollum, Dbovleir and Lake Timsah and back to Malta — which took about a month.

On the return of the aircraft to Felixstowe the Air Ministry placed a production order for 12 of these boats, to be called 'Scapa', and these equipped 202 and 204 Flying Boat Squadrons. Like its predecessor the Southampton, the Scapa undertook some long-distance cruises from the Mediterranean and they were involved in the Abyssinian confrontation with Italy in 1935. They also flew anti-submarine patrols in protection of neutral shipping during the Spanish Civil War, and they remained in RAF service until 1939.

So much impressed were Mitchell and Trevor Westbrook (General Manager of Supermarine) with George Pickering's handling of the Southampton IV at Felixstowe and the subsequent extended service trial based on Malta that they offered him the job of test pilot at Supermarine when his short service commission in the Royal Air Force expired in 1934.

George joined the company at Woolston in the middle of 1934 and he was therefore already well installed there when I joined very early in 1936.

By this time there was an active flying boat programme at Supermarine, for apart from the production order for the Scapa, a newer, higher performance, and somewhat larger boat, the Stranraer, with two Bristol Pegasus III M supercharged air-cooled engines of 820 hp, had been developed and ordered into production for the RAF, the prototype making its first flight on 27 July 1934.

Supermarine Aircraft since 1914, C.F. Andrews and E.B. Morgan (Putnam)

Production Stranraers had Pegasus X engines uprated to 920 hp which gave them a speed and climb performance unmatched by any other flying boat at the time.

Apart from the 17 Stranraers built at Woolston for delivery to the RAF, a licence was negotiated with Canadian Vickers of St Hubert, Montreal, for the production of 40 Stranraers for Canada.

These served with distinction throughout the war on both the Western and Eastern seaboards of Canada on anti-submarine patrols. The last Stranraer left RCAF service in January 1946.

Some Stranraers were acquired by Queen Charlotte Airlines of Vancouver after their RCAF service was over and the last one only retired from service as a civil aircraft relatively recently. It is now in the Canadian Aviation Museum in Ottawa, and there is one in the Royal Air Force Museum at Hendon.

Also, the Seagull V, the small single-engined amphibian in the trials of which George Pickering had been closely involved at Felixstowe, had been ordered into production as the Walrus, which was later destined for a distinguished wartime operational career in the Royal Navy and Royal Air Force, and in Australia, where it retained the name Seagull.

There had thus been a clear need in the firm in 1934 for a flying-boat pilot of the calibre of George Pickering. When the Spitfire production order was placed in June 1936 the Stranraer, and especially the Walrus contracts, were still in hand, and soon the design department was heavily engaged in the design of the B12/36 bomber as well as a new single-engined amphibian flying boat later to be called Sea Otter. So the company was already fairly well stretched by the time the Spitfire order was received and this goes a long way to explain the difficulties encountered initially with the Spitfire contract, described in Chapter 17.

When I arrived in the firm at the beginning of 1936 I was a fighter pilot pure and simple, both by training and by temperament, but I was very interested in sailing and was desperately keen to get some experience on flying boats.

> George was the acknowledged and undisputed expert on the marine side at Supermarine and I, in spite of my young age, was generally accepted as the 'Fighter boy'; but neither of us attempted to form any sort of a 'closed shop'. There had always been a certain mystique surrounding flying boats, but George Pickering, like the true expert that he was, would have none of this. As opportunities arose he taught me to fly them, concentrating on the essentials and dismissing the trivia. I was lucky to have my first introduction to flying boats from such a man.*

George and his wife Gladys lived in Southampton and they became personal friends of R.J. Mitchell and his wife and often spoke of their friendship and kindness and the interest they took in the Pickering children.

Spitfire: A Test Pilot's Story. Jeffrey Quill (John Murray, 1983)

George and Gladys also became good friends of mine and I look back with great nostalgia to my earliest days at Supermarine. I had always regarded George as a highly competent pilot of large flying boats and I used to wonder sometimes how he would take to a very advanced fighter like the Spitfire. He must have been getting on for thirty-three, which seemed to me then a vast age (I had learned to fly at eighteen and was now twenty-three), but somewhat to my surprise George, when he started to fly the Spitfire, took to it like a bird.

George was a very forthright and direct man with a salty turn of phrase when occasion demanded and he was very good at dealing with people of all sorts and was much liked and respected in the Works. I was still somewhat immature and diffident and only too happy to concentrate upon my flying and to leave much of the hassle and day-to-day problems on the ground to George to cope with.

In 1941 George suffered a catastrophic structural failure in a Spitfire V when diving it to its maximum permissible speed and he was desperately injured. It took him a year to recover from his injuries, only to be tragically killed in an accident in, of all things, a Bren Gun Carrier.

By this time the flying task at Supermarine had enormously expanded, we were employing more and more test pilots and the production testing needed a lot of organization, on top of which I was heavily engaged in the development programmes. I well remember the acute sense of loss that I experienced — a sort of loneliness — not to mention missing the fun of George's pungent comments on the passing scene from day to day.

CHAPTER 13

The First Flight

The prototype Spitfire was built in the Supermarine Works at Woolston, alongside the Floating Bridge, a chain ferry which plied back and forth across the River Itchen.

To prepare it for its first flight test, which would be carried out by Mutt Summers, the Chief Test Pilot of Vickers Aviation Ltd, the wings were removed and the fuselage, complete with engine, loaded on to a lorry and taken to Eastleigh aerodrome for re-erection. Here engine running and functional checks were carried out in the Supermarine hangar, of standard RFC pattern with wooden truss roof which was a relic of the First World War and is still in existence at what is now Southampton Airport.

The foreman who took charge of the aircraft during its final erection and throughout its subsequent flight tests was the late Ken Scales, a competent and very conscientious man who hardly let the aeroplane out of his sight, and attended it in a manner reminiscent of a head lad responsible for the welfare of a champion race-horse.

The great day came on 5 March. I flew Matt Summers to Eastleigh in the firm's Miles Falcon Six. The flight of F.37/34, Type 300, as yet unnamed and referred to within the firm simply as 'the Fighter', took place during the afternoon.

The aeroplane was unpainted and still in its Works finish of protective treatment on its metal surfaces, and its engine cowlings in natural but unpolished duralumin finish.

The prototype had been designed with a fixed-pitch, two-bladed wooden propeller for the good reason that a suitable variable-pitch propeller was not yet available in production in Britain, although de Havilland had negotiated a licence agreement with the Hamilton Standard Company in the USA. For the first flight, however, a special fine-pitch wooden propeller was fitted in order to give higher rpm for take-off and to minimize the somewhat unpredictable effect of torque reaction.

The weather was good with the wind blowing from just south of west, which meant that Mutt would have to take the shorter run across the aerodrome and so the precaution of fitting a finer-pitched propeller was no doubt a relief to both Mitchell and Mutt, for it ensured a safe take-off run.

Here follows a first-hand account of the event written by me as I was there:

There was a light wind blowing across the aerodrome which meant that Mutt had to take the short run and he taxied towards one of the four large Chance lights which (in those

The Spitfire prototype at Eastleigh as first flown on 5th March, 1936, with the large rudder balance

days) were situated round the perimeter, turned into wind and opened the throttle. The aeroplane was airborne after a very short run and climbed away comfortably. Mutt did not retract the undercarriage on that first flight — deliberately, of course — but cruised fairly gently around for some minutes, checked the lowering of the flaps and the slow flying and stalling characteristics, and then brought K5054 in to land. Although he had less room than he would probably have liked, he put the aeroplane down on three points without too much 'float', in which he was certainly aided by the fine-pitch setting of the propeller. He taxied towards the hangar and the point where we in the group of Supermarine spectators were standing. This included R.J. Mitchell, Alan Clifton, Beverley Shenstone, Alf Faddy, Ernest Mansbridge, 'Agony' Payn, Stuart Scott-Hall and Ken Scales, the foreman in charge of the aeroplane. There must also have been quite a few other people there but there was certainly not a crowd. It was very much a Supermarine 'family affair'.

When Mutt shut down the engine and everybody crowded round the cockpit, with R.J. foremost, Mutt pulled off his helmet and said firmly, 'I don't want anything touched.' This was destined to become a widely misinterpreted remark. What he meant was that there were no snags which required correction or adjustment before he flew the aircraft again. The remark has crept into folklore implying that the aeroplane was perfect in every respect from the moment of its first flight, an obviously absurd and impracticable idea. After the 15-minute

The slipstream from the large wooden propeller of the Spitfire Prototype required considerable weight on the tail to hold it down during engine runs. Standing by the wing, Ken Scales and Trevor Westbrook

first flight the aircraft was still largely untested and unproven, having done one take-off and one landing. Mutt was far too experienced a hand to make any such sweeping statement at that stage in the game.

However, it was a highly successful and encouraging first flight and Mutt Summers, with his experience of flying a great variety of prototype aircraft, was a highly shrewd judge of an aeroplane. By now I knew him well enough to see that he was obviously elated. Certainly to those of us watching from the ground 'the Fighter' in the air took on a very thoroughbred and elegant appearance, a strong but indefinable characteristic which was to remain with it throughout its long, varied and brilliantly successful life as a fighting aeroplane. Later that afternoon I flew Mutt back to Brooklands in the Falcon and we put the aircraft away and walked across to have a drink in Bob Lambert's well-known and congenial Brooklands Flying Club bar.* Mutt was pleased, obviously, to have one more successful first flight tucked under his belt, and I felt excited about this long, sleek and elegant machine which I knew that soon I would fly. A hundred yards from where Mutt and I were leaning against the bar was the hangar in which was standing K5083,

---

*A young student at the Chelsea Aeronautical Engineering College, Tom Brooke-Smith, was in the bar and remembers the occasion. He later became a distinguished test pilot carrying out early V.T.O.L. research flying, and also became Master of the Guild of Air Pilots and Air Navigators.

the prototype Hurricane, which had made its first flight in the hands of George Bulman some four months previously.

So the two new fighter aircraft — destined four years later to save our country in time of war — had now both flown in prototype form. Neither was yet anywhere near being a practical fighting machine nor was either yet ordered in quantity by the Royal Air Force, so much work still remained to be done.

To the old hands of the Supermarine design department who witnessed that event of 5 March 1936 it was just another first flight of a new type. They had seen many before, and while familiar with the feeling of achievement associated with a successful first flight and the guarded hopes and optimism for the future, they were also only too familiar with the failures, disappointment and frustration when results fell short of expectations. In other words they were professionals — their enthusiasm tempered by hard experience, and all too conscious that their previous fighter, embarked upon in the flush of confidence arising from their triumphs with the Schneider Trophy, had been something of a flop.

So there was no more than a modest atmosphere of celebration after the successful and safe conclusion of yet one more first flight

The prototype K5054, being flown by Jeffrey Quill. The excrescence ahead of the fin houses an anti-spin drag-chute – later removed

of a new type. Nevertheless the elegant beauty of the aeroplane in flight and particularly the air of confidence and optimism radiated by its test pilot, Mutt Summers, certainly raised most people's spirits. To me, young, enthusiastic, and inexperienced, it was an occasion of immense excitement and anticipation. None of us however on that day in March 1936 could possibly have sensed the true significance of what we had just witnessed nor anticipated the immense panorama of events that stretched ahead. The questions in most minds were how would the aeroplane perform when fully tested; what sort of trouble would we have with it; how would it compare with Sydney Camm's fighter from Hawkers; could we dare to hope for a production order from the Royal Air Force, and so on.

Meanwhile the international situation worsened still further for, two days after the Spitfire's first flight the German Army had reoccupied the demilitarized zone of the Rhineland in flagrant breach of the Versailles Treaty.

France and Britain, paralysed by political indecision and fatally committed to the policies of appeasement, did nothing. It is now known that had they shown any sign of military resistance the Germany army were under orders to withdraw at once. Thus the last chance of cheaply and effectively blocking Hitler's expansionist ambitions in Europe was thrown away and the Spitfire was born into the inevitability of war.

However in the most secret of circles of Government in London the gloom engendered by Stanley Baldwin's prediction to Parliament (1933) that 'the bomber would always get through' had given way to a cautious optimism that perhaps the bomber need *not* always get through. Experiments started by Dr (later Sir Robert) Watson-Watt in February 1935 had led to the invention of RDF (later to be called radar). It was still very much in its infancy, but by March 1936 the experimental station set up at Bawdsey on the coast of Suffolk was able to report that it had tracked an aircraft out over the sea to a distance of 75 miles. Hopes were being expressed that soon it would be possible to measure accurately the distance and bearing of incoming aircraft at a range of 50 miles. This was a breakthrough of incalculable importance.

There is something rather uncanny — almost redolent of divine intervention — about that month of March 1936 which saw the birth of the Spitfire and the concurrent discovery of the key element which would enable it, and the Hurricane, to do the job for which they were designed so very much more effectively.

CHAPTER 14

Joseph 'Mutt' Summers

Joseph 'Mutt' Summers had been Chief Test Pilot for Vickers (Aviation) Ltd since 1928, when he had been appointed as a result of the death of 'Tiny' Scholefield who had been killed at Brooklands testing a civil aircraft called the Vanguard.

At the time Mutt was just coming to the end of a short service commission in the Royal Air Force and was serving as a test pilot at the Aeroplane and Armament Experimental Establishment at Martlesham Heath (the forerunner of Boscombe Down). When Scholefield was killed, Mutt applied for the job and got it, and his appointment roughly coincided with the take-over of Supermarine by Vickers (Aviation) Ltd. Mutt had acquired a good reputation as a pilot in the RAF and had been engaged in test flying duties at Martlesham and was therefore a sound choice by Vickers.

'Mutt' Summers

Concurrently Henri Biard was coming to the end of his flying life at Supermarine and no replacement was in mind, so Sir Robert McLean put Mutt in charge of the flying at both firms.

This was a wise decision of McLean's for it is never easy to integrate the operations of two companies after a take-over of one by the other, unless the most ruthless methods are employed which are usually detrimental to the firm taken over. There could be no question of integrating the two design departments, thus destroying the autonomy of one of them, because the acquisition of Mitchell and his team was one of the principal objectives of the purchase and the design situation at Weybridge was entirely satisfactory and healthy under Rex Pierson whose standing was very high with the Air Ministry.

Neither was it possible to integrate the operations of the Works beyond a limited extent, such as placing sub-contracts with each other rather than outside, although McLean soon appointed the 'high-flyer' from Weybridge, Trevor Westbrook, to take charge of the Works at Supermarine in the capacity of General Manager.

One thing that could be done, however, was to integrate the test flying under a common head, Mutt Summers. This, it was hoped, would do much to bring the two companies together and foster a sense of common objective.

Because Mutt joined Vickers (Aviation) and Supermarine at a time when prototype aircraft were built quickly and frequently he was able to cram in a vast amount of experience of testing a wide variety of prototype aircraft in a comparatively short time. By the time he retired in 1951, and as recorded in the books on Vickers and Supermarine aircraft by C. F. Andrews and E. B. Morgan, (Putnam), Summers had carried out the first flights and initial test programmes of some 30 prototypes in his 22 years as Vickers Chief Test Pilot.

Mutt Summers was very much a child of his own aviation generation which was very different from that which we have become accustomed to today. Flying in the 1920s and early 1930s was still very much a 'seat of the pants' affair, although there had been substantial technological advances since the end of World War I.

As far as test flying was concerned the techniques of measuring the performance of aircraft by accurate and scientific methods was well established, with Martlesham and Farnborough setting the pace. There had also been considerable progress in the development of accurate instrumentation carried in aircraft, and piloting techniques had evolved accordingly.

However, the business of assessing the handling qualities of aircraft in the air was still almost entirely dependent upon qualitative judgement by the test pilot. Practically no instrumentation existed even for the accurate measurement of control forces or control displacements. Some accelerometers existed but were seldom fitted. The theory of aircraft stability in flight was largely an academic study; spinning was still something of a bogeyman surviving from the First War, although all fighter aircraft were required to demonstrate good recovery characteristics from an eight-turn spin in each direction.

Structural failures in the air, due to wing flutter, aileron flutter or some other cause of overstressing the structure, were common and very much uppermost in most test pilots' minds during the trials of newly designed prototypes. While engines had made vast strides in reliability since the close of the First War, power failure in the air, particularly in the course of performance testing (which demanded running the engine at full power for prolonged periods), was a very frequent hazard, and much progress was still to be made in the matter of reliable and fireproof fuel systems and engine installations generally.

The test pilot of those days had essentially to be a skilful and reliable handler of an aeroplane and to have a good knowledge of the machine and the engines he was testing in all their aspects so as to react to emergencies in an immediate and intelligent manner. He had to be a good judge of the aircraft's handling qualities and fitness for purpose, to be meticulously observant, and above all able to establish a rapport with the designers and to understand their problems and difficulties so as to raise the quality of communication.

The test pilot was, and still is, essentially a bridge between the rather abstruse technological world of the designers and technicians and the very different world of the operator, be he fighter pilot, bomber pilot, airline pilot or whatever. The really successful test pilot gains the best understanding he can of both sides of the equation.

I am not saying that Mutt Summers was a paragon in all these respects, but he went some way towards it. That he was an exceedingly skilful pilot and a shrewd judge of an aeroplane is not in doubt. The record speaks for itself.

CHAPTER 15

Martlesham and the Production Order

After the first flight Mutt Summers made a few more flights, devoted principally to checking the handling and general functioning characteristics before K5054 went back into the shops to receive a covering of high-gloss paint of a pale grey/blue colour.

Mutt soon handed the aeroplane over to George Pickering and me to complete performance trials and the schedule of contractor's trials before it went to Martlesham for its official Air Ministry acceptance trials.

From the outset K5054 was a pleasure to fly and at first sight its performance seemed exciting. Nevertheless the first set of accurately measured performance trials, which I carried out on 27 March, were disappointing, yielding a maximum true speed of little more than 335 mph at less than 17,000 feet.

Mitchell had set his heart on the estimated speed of 350 mph with the Merlin 'C' engine then installed. Clearly there must be some reason for the disappointing speed performance and RJ would not allow the aircraft to go to Martlesham for its official trials until the causes were identified and corrected and the aeroplane achieving a speed of 350 mph.

The prototype Spitfire in war paint at Eastleigh

The grapevine was telling us at Supermarine that the prototype Hurricane, already at Martlesham, was showing a true speed of around 325 mph.

The Hurricane was an aircraft designed with ease of production very much in mind. It was constructed on the lines developed by Hawkers during the days of the Hart and the Fury. With some justification it was sometimes referred to as the 'monoplane Fury', and its production was therefore something which the Hawker factories could tackle with confidence. It was a fine aircraft, but it was also larger than the Spitfire, and mostly fabric-covered.

The Spitfire, on the other hand, was technologically a much more advanced stressed-skin structure and would certainly be difficult and probably expensive to produce in quantity in the industry of those days. Furthermore, the Air Staff were undoubtedly looking to Mitchell and Supermarine, with all their Schneider experience behind them, to produce something of outstanding performance. Indeed unless the Spitfire offered some very substantial speed advantage over the Hurricane it was unlikely to be ordered into production. Thus the disappointing speed performance of our prototype at that early stage was something of a crisis and Mitchell was a very worried man.

Steps were taken to 'clean up' the aircraft in various ways and to try to identify any hidden sources of drag, but this produced no more than marginal improvement. Then suspicion fell upon the fixed-pitch wooden propeller when it was realized that at the true speed which the Spitfire was achieving at 18,000 feet the helical speed of the propeller tips was penetrating well into the compressibility region. In other words it was in Mach Number trouble.

A new propeller was designed at Supermarine with modified tip sections and this was first flown on 27 March by me. E.H. Mansbridge who was the performance engineer supervising the flight tests of the prototype is quoted by Alfred Price* as follows:

> Jeffrey went off and did a set of level speeds with it. When he came down he handed me the test card with a big grin and said 'I think we've got something here.' And we had — we'd got 13 mph. After correcting the figures we made the maximum speed 348 mph, which we were very pleased with.

Mitchell was satisfied with this speed and so was prepared to let the aircraft go to Martlesham. At this point we had already completed most of the essential test work required before delivery, such as proving the suitability of cooling and oil systems and the completion of dives to the maximum design speeds and generally proving the integrity of the structure. It remained for us finally to clear the handling to a standard likely to be acceptable to Martlesham, and this meant, among other things, establishing the centre of gravity limits by a qualitative assessment of the longitudinal stability behaviour.

---

*The Spitfire Story. Alfred Price (Ian Allan)

The prototype Spitfire with its eight machine-guns fitted

All our tests so far had shown the stability of the Spitfire to be very sensitive to rearward movements of the centre of gravity and the handling on the ground was also sensitive to forward movements thereof. We had to resort to ballasting to obtain a satisfactory compromise and this was signalling a problem which was to be endemic to the Spitfire through its future development life.

However the stability characteristics were satisfactory for immediate purposes and on 26 May 1936 K5054 was flown to RAF Martlesham Heath by Mutt Summers.

'A' Flight at the A & AEE (the Fighter Flight) was commanded by Flt. Lieut. Humphrey Edwardes-Jones who thus became the first Royal Air Force officer to fly the Spitfire, on 26 May 1936, the day it was delivered.

An extraordinary and probably unique circumstance in the history of that famous Establishment is that on 3 June, only seven days after it was first delivered and when it had done a minimum of official test flying, and before any formal report had been submitted to Air Ministry, a production contract for 310 aircraft was placed with Supermarine.

Under the stimulus of the pressure and enthusiasm of Sqn. Ldr. Ralph Sorley of the Operational Requirements Branch, and the shrewd judgement of Air Marshal Sir Wilfrid Freeman, the Air Member for Research and Development, the Air Council had made up its mind in advance that it would order the Spitfire provided it could be satisfied on two vital points: first, that the aircraft was achieving its design top speed of 350 mph; and second, that it could safely be flown by the ordinary Service-trained pilot.

They knew from the performance results obtained by Supermarine, before delivery to Martlesham, that the aircraft was

Air Marshal Sir Ralph Sorley who, as a Squadron Leader in the Air Ministry operational requirements branch in 1935 recommended the fitting of eight machine guns in the forthcoming Spitfire and Hurricane interceptor fighters.

achieving just on 350 mph at about 17,000 feet, but they could not be satisfied on the second point until they could have the opinion of an experienced and competent Service test pilot, and for this they had to wait for the arrival of the aircraft at Martlesham.

Before Mutt Summers and the Spitfire arrived at Martlesham, which was in the late afternoon, Edwardes Jones, or E.J. as he was universally known, had received orders, through his immediate C.O. Squadron Leader Ted Hilton, that he was to fly the Spitfire as soon as it arrived and thereafter was to telephone Air Marshal Sir Wilfrid Freeman at his office in the Air Ministry. No reason for this was given to E.J. at the time.

This involved a considerable departure from the normal routine at Martlesham, which was that when a new aircraft arrived, whether civil or military, it would at once pass into the hands of the 'boffins' who would scrutinize it thoroughly, weigh it accurately, calibrate its flight instruments and probably add some instrumentation of their own such as recording barographs etc. to facilitate the performance trials. It might be anything up to a week or ten days before the Technical and Scientific Departments released the aircraft for the test pilots to fly.

In this case, however, the Spitfire was immediately refuelled and after a short cockpit briefing E.J. flew it at once as instructed. On landing he rang Sir Wilfrid Freeman at the Air Ministry, unaware of what was the reason for the call. Sir Wilfrid said that he was fully aware that E.J. could not give any detailed information about the aircraft after only one flight; he was, however, interested in only one question and would like a straight answer to it: was the aeroplane, in E.J.'s opinion, capable of being flown safely by the ordinary Service-trained fighter pilot, more particularly those emerging from the training sequence being set up to meet the new expansion programmes?

By any standards this was a pretty fast ball for a senior Air Marshal to bowl at a Flight-Lieutenant just emerging from the cockpit of a new and strange type of aircraft after his first flight in it.

Fortunately for us all, and to his great credit, E.J. answered with an unequivocal 'yes'. Pilots emerging from the current training system, he reported, provided they were adequately instructed in the use of retractable undercarriages, flaps, and other systems of the new types of aircraft coming into RAF service, would have no difficulty with the Spitfire which was 'a delight to fly'.

This judgement was undoubtedly right but in the circumstances it was a bold judgement.

Had E.J. said 'No', or 'maybe', or otherwise hedged his bet, it would have resulted in other pilots being consulted and no doubt an endless evaluation process and endless arguments. But E.J. said 'yes', and that was the end of it. One week later, 3 June, the production contract was placed.

Clearly the Air Council had been extremely keen to get the order placed — no doubt for good departmental reasons associated with the availability of finance — and had there been any serious delay in placing the order it would certainly have compounded the problems of getting the Spitfire into production (described in Chapter 17), and so might well have resulted in there being fewer Spitfires available at the outbreak of the Battle of Britain some four years later.

Another interesting aspect of the Spitfire's first arrival at Martlesham was recently described by Edwardes Jones. As indicated earlier, new aircraft arrivals were commonplace and excited little attention or comment in that sophisticated Establishment. The arrival of the Spitfire on that 26 May, however, created a quite extraordinary amount of interest at Martlesham. While E.J. was airborne on his first flight, which was in the evening when the aerodrome was normally closed down, the word had evidently got around the station that the Spitfire had arrived. So when E.J. returned and circled the aerodrome prior to landing and looked down he was surprised to see a large and unaccustomed throng of people assembled on the tarmac. He also noticed the white caps of the duty cooks outside the airmen's cookhouse, who had turned out to watch the Spitfire's approach.

This was perhaps a very early manifestation of the remarkable magnetism or charisma that the Spitfire possessed and still retains after fifty years.

Perhaps it was due to the glamour of its immediate ancestors, the Schneider Trophy racers and world record holders; or to the great reputation of its designer; or to its undoubted beauty of line; or the inspiring note of its Merlin engine. More probably it was a subtle combination of all these factors, added to which was the fact that at Martlesham Heath at that time officers and airmen alike were deeply conscious that a new generation of fighters was on the way, setting new standards of performance and lethality, and that in them was vested the future security of the country in an increasingly dangerous world, as well as the future of the Royal Air Force.

CHAPTER 16

Sir Thomas Inskip

The production orders for 600 Hurricanes and 310 Spitfires, which were signed on 3 June 1936, were placed under the overall authority of the RAF expansion Scheme 'F' which had been approved by the Cabinet in February 1936. Scheme 'F' called for, among other things, 20 heavy bomber, 48 medium bomber, and 20 fighter squadrons (10 of the last destined for work with the planned Army Field Force).

Scheme 'F' was, of course, eventually superseded by further and more comprehensive expansion schemes as the re-armament situation developed.

In retrospect, and in view of the fact that eventually more than 14,000 Hurricanes and 22,000 Spitfires and Seafires were produced, it is perhaps remarkable that these initial orders were so modest. In June 1936 however the British re-armament programmes were evolving somewhat tentatively within the constraints of a peace-time economy and there were still pious hopes of solving or ameliorating the problem of Hitler's Germany by diplomatic means. Moreover there were still grey areas of doubt and uncertainty about how the aircraft industry could respond to the challenges of the immediate future.

By 1937 the cost of the re-armament programmes was causing serious anxiety about its overall effect on the British economy. Up to 30% of the cost of re-armament lay in the price of imported raw materials and this was having a very serious effect on the balance of payments which had only recently recovered from the effects of 1931.

The new Chancellor of the Exchequer, Sir John Simon, started sounding alarm bells which resulted in a major review of defence expenditure in the summer of 1937. From this it became clear that the projected programmes of the Navy, the Army and the Air Force could not be met, as Simon pointed out, without some risk of bankrupting the country.

Accordingly, Sir Thomas Inskip,* the newly appointed Minister for the Co-ordination of Defence, was instructed by the Cabinet to examine the programmes put forward by the three Services with a view to reducing their total cost. Sir Thomas was a lawyer who had in the past occupied the post of Attorney-General and he made no claim to any specialized knowledge of military affairs, but he applied a very logical and analytical mind to the problem.

His recommendations for economies, not suprisingly, did not

---

*Later created first Viscount Caldecote.

find favour with the Admiralty, the War Office or the Air Ministry, but here we are concerned primarily with his attitudes as they affected the Air Force. Here it should be said that Chamberlain, the Prime Minister, believed that the Navy and the Air Force should get the lion's share of defence expenditure and the Foreign Office, under Eden, insisted that air parity with Germany was an essential pillar of policy in Europe. However Inskip's job was to examine, or question, the individual programmes of the three Services in detail.

The Air Staff, strongly influenced by Trenchardian doctrines of air power, considered that a force of fighters for the close defence of the United Kingdom would be of limited effectiveness and that the main instrument of defence against a concerted air attack would be a counter-force of bombers which would strike back at the enemy, thus taking the edge off his assault. The possibility that the Germans were preparing to launch a 'knock-out' blow from the air was considered a likely eventuality for which provision had to be made. Hence Scheme 'J', then in draft, called for a greatly increased force of heavy bombers, and for bombers to have priority over fighters, in accordance with the Air Staff's general philosophy that attack was the best method of defence.

Inskip's study was heading him towards an examination of the relative costs of a counter-offensive bomber force and a close defence fighter force and in December 1937 he produced an *aide memoire* in which he challenged the whole counter-offensive concept:

> The role of the RAF had never been to launch a knock-out blow, only to prevent the enemy trying one. Britain, on the contrary, must be able to confront the Germans with the risk of a long war, which superior British staying-power, based on her economic resources, would assuredly win . . .
>
> If Britain adopted such a strategy there would be no need for the RAF to have as many long-range bombers as the Germans at the beginning of a war; it would make no military sense . . . The security of the home country was the essential pre-requisite and victory would be won by attrition in a long war. The RAF was to fit into this traditional strategy, first by providing close fighter defence in the early stages of the war and second by providing the bomber force which would act as a supplement to the traditional mechanism of attrition in British strategy, maritime blockade.*

On the basis of this argument for a strong fighter defence in the initial stages followed by the build-up of a powerful bomber counter-force later, Inskip proposed priority for the fighter force under Scheme 'J' and the postponement of the bomber programme.

British Air Strategy Betweeen the Wars, Dr Malcolm Smith (OUP).

The huge Castle Bromwich Shadow factory, full of Spitfire IIs in 1940

Rather naturally this provoked a sharp reaction from the Air Staff of the day, for not only was Inskip attacking their basic philosophies based on Trenchardian doctrines but there was no guarantee that a defence based primarily on fighters would be effective — indeed previous experience suggested it would not — and furthermore it was by no means sure that the reorganized and newly galvanized Nazi Germany of Adolf Hitler would be vulnerable to attritional warfare.

Inskip's arguments in 1937, although conflicting with the Air Staff's ideas, made a considerable impression upon a Cabinet trying to counter the threat from Germany without destroying the British economy or dangerously disrupting British industry as a whole.

Without doubt Inskip was responsible for initiating a shift in priority from bombers to fighters, although the major shift in emphasis came a little later with Scheme 'L' drawn up after the *Anschluss* with Austria and Scheme 'M' drawn up in the aftermath of Munich.

So by a peculiarly British process of argument and counter-argument against a background of hard economic, industrial and political pressures the right answer was found. In the event the calculated risk of placing so much reliance upon a fighter defence paid off because, in the nick of time, a fighter control and command system based on a chain of RDF (radar) stations, and two magnificent new fighter aircraft were ready at the time of the attempted knock-out blow — the Battle of Britain.

Stanley Woodley, Works Manager at the enormous Castle Bromwich Shadow factory

Thus the influence of Sir Thomas Inskip, the quiet lawyer, during his term of office as Minister for Co-ordination of Defence in the Chamberlain Government, was to be of profound importance to the country.

By 1937 the Government had embarked upon schemes for shadow factories which would increase the country's war potential by providing greatly increased production capacity which the aircraft industry could not possibly provide on its own. These factories would produce chosen aircraft in large numbers under direct Government contract, and it was at about this time that Lord Swinton, the Air Minister, started discussions with Lord Nuffield, the Head of the automobile firm Morris Motors Ltd, on the construction of a great factory at Castle Bromwich which was to produce fighters (initially Westland Whirlwinds were considered) in large quantities, and in due course, bomber aircraft.

In March 1939 it was decided that Castle Bromwich should produce Spitfires and not Whirlwinds and a contract for 1,000 aircraft was placed on 12 April 1939. Production of Spitfires at Castle Bromwich (under the management of Vickers-Armstrong) to augment the output of the Supermarine factories, commenced in June 1940 and soon Castle Bromwich became the largest single source of Spitfire production, achieving a maximum rate of output of nearly 350 Spitfires a month in 1943.

Later it also produced Lancaster bombers and so events at Castle Bromwich followed closely the pattern of Inskip's logically calculated priorities.

CHAPTER 17

Into Production

Air Ministry Contract 527113/36 for 310 Spitfire Mk Is stipulated that delivery should commence in October 1937 and that the contract should be completed by March 1939. The earliest forecast made by the firm, (but some while before the contract was signed) was that delivery could commence in May 1937. Spitfire production, however, was to prove a major headache for both the Air Council and Supermarine for the next four years, and relations between Sir Robert McLean and the members of the Council were embittered by the controversy which raged.

In the last six months of 1936 the first signs that all might not go smoothly on the production side began to surface. The Air Ministry's progress report of September 1936 for the Defence Policy Requirements Sub-Committee of the Committee of Imperial Defence gave estimated delivery figures of 20 aircraft per month commencing in October 1937 as planned. In the following month's report the first doubts about Supermarine's estimates began to appear with the statement that 'DAP [Director of Aeronautical Production] doubts if more than 15 a month will be delivered.' Nevertheless, slippages in aircraft production programmes were not uncommon and did not give rise to undue concern as long as they did not become serious. That at least one member of the Air Council believed that Supermarine's programme of aircraft production was overly ambitious, and that this would cause serious problems, is revealed by the following extract from the Minutes of the Secretary of State for Air's progress meeting for 28 July 1936:

Lord Weir [Indusrial Adviser to the Secretary of State for Air] said that the remark on A.M. Form 1407* that work on the Spitfire was 'proceeding according to schedule' had now appeared for several weeks, and he would like a rather more informative report . . . What was the schedule? . . It struck him that Supermarine's programme was very large in relation to the size of their works, and he would like to be sure that their capacity had been carefully examined before their share of the programme had been decided upon. They had contracts for Seagulls, Walruses, and Stranraers, all running simultaneously, in the latter part of 1936 and early 1937, and were due to start on the Spitfire in the autumn of 1937. This was a considerable undertaking.

---

*A.M. Form 1407 was submitted by the aircraft firms to the Air Ministry giving the latest production estimates.

Sir Robert McLean. Chairman, Vickers (Aviation) Ltd, and the Supermarine Aviation Works (Vickers) Ltd

Other members of the Air Council promptly reassured Lord Weir that all these factors had been taken into account before the order had been placed, but his concern was to prove well founded.

In April 1937 Supermarine told the Air Ministry that they expected to deliver the first four aircraft in December 1937, and then build up production to an average of 20 per month with the last two aircraft being delivered in July 1939, just three months behind schedule. The revised programme came about as a result of intense pressure from the Air Ministry for Supermarine to further sub-contract Spitfire production. Following a visit to Supermarine's Southampton works by the Director of Aeronautical Production in January 1937 it had been suggested to Sir Robert McLean that further work should be placed in the hands of sub-contractors, particularly General Aircraft Ltd, who were already manufacturing complete tail units. Sir Robert McLean had refused this request, but instead had offered to increase Spitfire production by reducing the monthly output of Walruses. This suggestion palpably increased the Air Council's exasperation with Sir Robert McLean as they suspected, possibly correctly, that he wished to retain as much as he could of the Spitfire production work at Supermarine. This action led Lord Swinton to describe the situation with regard to the Spitfire as 'disgraceful' and 'intolerable', and to consider summoning the Vickers Board of Directors before the Air Council to make clear their concern. The Air Council's determination on this point and the weakness of

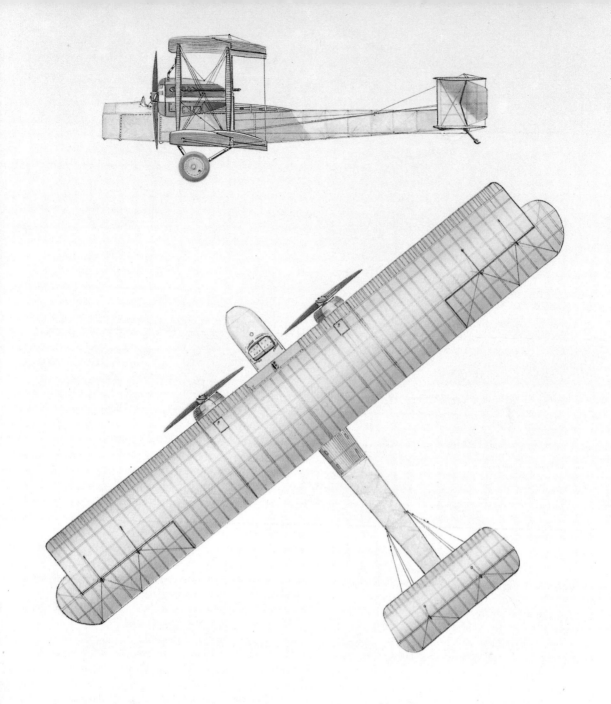
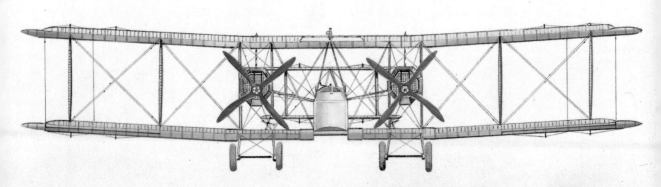

PREVIOUS PAGE: *The Vickers Vimy of Alcock and Brown, 1919.*

ABOVE: *Supermarine Southampton flying boats of the RAF Far East Flight over Singapore harbour, 1927. A painting by Alan Fearnley.*

LEFT: *The Curtiss CR-3 of Lt. David Rittenhouse USN, who finished 1st in the 1923 Schneider Trophy contest at Cowes, Isle of Wight. Painting by Kenneth McDonough.*

SUPERMARINE S6
Frank Munger AMRAeS G.Av.A for AEROPLANE MONTHLY 1976

ABOVE: *Gerald Coulson's emotive painting of the Spitfire prototype K5054.*

LEFT: *Spitfire VB's over the Solent. Painting by Roger Steel.*

RIGHT: *General arrangement painting by John W. Wood of a Spitfire F.XIVe*

John W. Wood
© 1984

Supermarine's position forced Sir Robert McLean to agree to further sub-contracting. Approximately 80% of initial Spitfire production was eventually sub-contracted.

Sub-contracting, however, did not prove quite the panacea the Air Council had hoped. Sir Robert McLean wrote in April 1937 making it clear that Supermarine could only keep to its revised production schedule if the sub-contractors also kept to their delivery dates, and it is quite clear that in this respect the sub-contractors did not fulfil their expectations. The reason for this, however, is far from clear, although it certainly appears that a large measure of the blame must again be laid at Supermarine's door. Thus, despite the fact that Sir Robert McLean placed the fault squarely on the sub-contractors, a meeting at the Air Ministry in April 1937 found that in the case of at least two of the major sub-contractors, namely General Aircraft (tail units) and Beaton and Sons (wings), 'the allegation was entirely without foundation, except in regard to deliveries of raw materials, for the ordering of which Supermarine were responsible'. Deliveries of raw materials from Supermarine to sub-contractors were still 'very badly behind' at the beginning of June. The extent to which the raw material suppliers were responsible for this state of affairs is not known.

Nor was this the only problem between Supermarine and the sub-contractors. The latter also complained bitterly that they had not received from Supermarine many of the component drawings which they required to start manufacture. When these drawings were received they were often found to be less than accurate: that there was much truth in these complaints is evinced by the fact that General Aircraft preferred a claim for £40,000 on the grounds that the delays in the provision of accurate drawings had resulted in a serious hold-up in the production of Spitfire components. The truth was of course, as Lord Weir had perceived, that Supermarine, with substantial orders for Walruses, Stranraers and Spitfires, was seriously over-stretched. Thus, when the drawing-office was required to produce sets of component drawings for sub-contractors they found it difficult to meet the deadlines and quality inevitably suffered. The size and complexity of the task facing Supermarine's draughtsmen is nicely illustrated by the following quote from one of their number, Jack Davis: 'The task of redoing the drawings took about a year. One couldn't conveniently use prototype drawings for the production aircraft, there were so many changes. Though some of the production drawings might have looked the same as those for the prototype, it was much better to redraw and renumber the whole lot.'*

This meant that some thousands of new drawings had to be produced for the Mark I, and good draughtsmen were in short supply.

The problems between Supermarine and the sub-contractors rumbled on through the early part of 1938 with the Air Council becoming increasingly frustrated by the lack of solid progress.

The Spitfire Story, by Alfred Price

This sense of frustration was undoubtedly compounded by Supermarine's apparent inability to keep them fully informed. Throughout 1937 the firm continued to submit the same revised estimate that they had been compelled to submit in April despite the manifest problems with production. In 1938 the company simply resorted to stating that they could not forcast deliveries 'at present'. In February 1938 the Air Council felt constrained to make a further attempt to sort out the mess. The catalyst was a statement on A.M. Form 1407 which revealed that a shortage of certain Spitfire components manufactured by the firm of Deritends was again holding up production. This rather transparent attempt to shift the blame for further delays on to yet another sub-contractor prompted Lord Swinton, who was well aware that it was the lack of completed wings which was the prime cause of the production setbacks, to inquire whether any information could be produced on their availability. The DAP 'replied in the negative; the wings were admittedly very difficult to make but there had been constant trouble with the two firms [General Aircraft and Pobjoy] who were making both the port and starboard wings, though the parent firm were to some extent to blame on account of the number of corrections to drawings which they were still sending out'.

Swinton swiftly decided to arrange a meeting with Sir Charles Craven, the Managing Director of Vickers-Armstrong Ltd. One week later the Air Council was informed of the results of the meeting. Sir Charles had agreed that the sub-contracting arrangements had been badly managed and he had stated that he was doing his best to improve matters in this respect. He was satisfied that the layout of the Southampton factory was efficient and he felt that once the firm started getting wings from their sub-contractors they ought to be able to work up to an average of 17 or even 20 Spitfires per month.

The reactions of the members of the Air Council to these statements are not recorded in the minutes, but they must by now have felt that they had heard it all before, and indeed they were to hear it all again only one month later, in April 1938. By this date, however, the problem was no longer one of drawings and raw materials, but rather the supply of small components from Supermarine to the sub-contractors. The minutes of the Air Council meeting have a familiar and depressing ring to them:

> AMRD [Air Member for Research and Development, Sir Wilfrid Freeman] said the real trouble appeared to lie in the chaotic state of the firm's sub-contracting arrangements. Several of the sub-contractors were becoming exasperated by delays by Vickers in providing them with the parts without which they could not complete their sub-contracting work. For example, there were 60 or 70 tail-planes lying at Short's Works awaiting details and in several instances when the necessary parts had been received from the parent firm it was found that they would not fit.

The real problem, however, remained the manufacture of the

wings. An assurance from Supermarine that four Spitfires would be delivered in June remained unfulfilled; yet another in a long line of such broken promises, and when the Air Member for Development and Production and the Director General of Pro- duction* visited the Southampton works they found 78 fuselages but only 3 sets of wings. Instructions were issued that additional jigs for wings were to be prepared by Supermarine themselves for the manufacture of these crucial items. Additional jigs were also to be prepared for General Aircraft. In fact it would appear from Vickers' own records that duplicate wing jigs were already being prepared at Woolston as early as March 1938, and that 35 fuselages and 4 sets of wings were ready in that month. Similarly the Supermarine quarterly report for the Vickers Board dated 30 June 1938 stated that 80 fuselages were complete at Eastleigh, but only 12 sets of wings.

Nevertheless, whatever the true picture with regard to the supply of wings (and it seems likely that Supermarine figures were more accurate than the impressions of visiting Air Council mem- bers), the situation was about to take a turn for the better. If the change was not dramatic it did indicate that perhaps the worst of the problems were past. On 15 May 1938 the first production Spitfire, K9787, made its maiden flight with Jeffrey Quill at the controls. However, the second aircraft, K9788, did not take to the air until 12 July, and the lengthy series of test flights necessary on K9788 by Supermarine's test pilots meant that the first aircraft was not delivered until 17 July 1938. This was actually K9788, which went initially to Rolls-Royce at Hucknall, but was accepted on charge to the Air Member for Development and Production's Department on that date. On the 29 July K9792 was flown to the Central Flying School at Upavon, where Flt. Lt. George Stainforth AFC, of Schneider Trophy fame, accepted it as the first aircraft to enter service directly with the Royal Air Force. It was on 4 August that perhaps the most significant delivery took place, when Jeffrey Quill landed K9789 at Duxford for delivery to No. 19 Squadron; the first Spitfire to enter squadron service. It was a red-letter day indeed, and the streamlined beauty of K9789 standing alongside the biplane Gloster Gauntlets, with which at that time 19 and 66 Squadrons were still equipped, revealed how great the pace of change had been since the RAF's very first Gauntlet had been delivered to 19 Squadron in February 1935, just three and a half years earlier. If any of those present spared a moment to think of the significance of the international political events unfolding in Europe they must have felt that the new aircraft had arrived not a moment too soon.

These early deliveries did not solve the production difficulties of the Spitfires, but the most intractable of them were now past, and whilst production accelerated only slowly, and further prob- lems remained to be overcome, the Spitfire was eventually to form the backbone of the RAF's fighter force until 1945.

---

*Sir Wilfrid Freeman and Sir Ernest Lemon. The visit must have taken place in June or early July.

It is perhaps of value to consider these early production problems as dispassionately as possible, and to place them firmly in their pre-war context rather than viewing them with the benefit of hindsight perhaps influenced by the production triumphs of the war years. It must first of all be admitted that Supermarine and Vickers do not emerge from the affair with untarnished reputations. Sir Robert McLean's early production estimates were undoubtedly grossly optimistic, and it seems highly likely that he knew them to be so from the start. Worse perhaps were the apparent attempts to disguise the true gravity of the situation from the Air Council, and of continuing to make optimistic promises of delivery as late as June 1938. This led to increasing frustration and fury in the ranks of the Air Council which, ultimately, did Supermarine and Sir Robert McLean more harm than good, particularly as the latter was in trouble with Wellington production at Vickers Weybridge.

These faults and errors on the part of Supermarine and Vickers are by no means the whole story, and in order to appreciate the underlying causes of the production failures it is necessary to consider briefly the historical trends in aircraft production between the wars, and the crucial role played by the Air Ministry and successive Governments in the development of aviation during that period. Throughout the 1920s all three Services had had to

The prototype Spitfire in warpaint and with guns mounted.

struggle to survive in an atmosphere of severe financial retrenchment, exemplified by the infamous Ten Year Rule, a Treasury edict which assumed that no major European war would break out for at least a decade. The Ten Year Rule was moved forward on a rolling basis year by year until its final abandonment in 1929, exactly ten years before the outbreak of the Second World War. This policy effectively prevented the Services from planning any modernization of their equipment, or indeed any proper consideration of their tasks in a major war. Matters did not improve very much with the abandonment of this policy in 1929 since military aviation then became a prime target for the Geneva Disarmament Conference and was, ludicrously, threatened with abolition. No responsible Government of course was about to waste money developing an item which might be outlawed at any moment. Add to these factors the severe economic depression of the early 1930s and it is easy to understand why money for aviation was so critically short.

In these circumstances the Air Ministry adopted a policy of spreading orders, such as they were, very thinly between the sixteen major airframe manufacturers, in order to try and preserve the firms' design teams and industrial capacity intact. In so far as the major firms were all still functioning in 1935, and all had established strong links with the Air Ministry, this policy was successful. However, it had in many cases been a close-run thing and several firms had been on the verge of bankruptcy; Westland for instance had resorted to making stainless steel barrels in order to survive, and Supermarine mahogany lavatory seats, no doubt with the skilled craftsmen who built the Southampton's wooden hulls. In such circumstances even successful and innovative designs often received only very modest production orders. It is hardly surprising, therefore, that in the changed circumstances of the late 1930s the manufacturers, Supermarine amongst them, were still not prepared to take risks by greatly expanding their production facilities and employing more labour without direct pressure from the Air Ministry. Still less, when the large expansion scheme orders started to arrive, were they prepared to see a third of the work go out to sub-contractors, largely from other industries, who had not had to struggle to make ends meet during the years of depression. While with the benefit of hindsight we can see the awful inevitability of war at least from 1938 onwards, many manufacturers must have been haunted by fears that the tension would ease, and that in consequence drastic reduction or cancellation of the massive orders being placed by the Air Ministry would soon follow. Thus, a natural desire to enjoy to the full the fruits of the expanded order books, combined with doubt that it might prove anything more than a temporary phenomenon, served to encourage the aircraft firms to keep as much of the expanded production to themselves as possible.

The state of the British aviation industry at that time goes a long way towards explaining why it was that Sir Robert McLean's initial production forecasts were unduly optimistic. The industry had thus existed at a bare subsistence level for many years. The few small-scale foreign orders had not been enough to extend production runs, which had remained short and uncertain. The industry had thus become accustomed to a system of manufacture which allowed for small production batches, with the maximum scope for flexibility in making modifications or design changes. Supermarine was also one of the smaller aircraft firms, employing only 1,370 people in June 1936, and the longest production run in the firm's history prior to the Spitfire had been the orders for 79 Southamptons placed in batches over an eight-year period. Moreover, even the larger firms such as Hawker, who had enjoyed longer production runs than most with the Hart and Fury variants, were unable to meet the Air Ministry's rapidly burgeoning demand for aircraft in the late 1930s. Thus similar delays occurred in Hurricane production, despite the fact that Camm's fighter required a less sophisticated manufacturing technique than the more technologically advanced Spitfire. It is in fact no great exaggeration to say that few, if any, of the large production orders placed with the aircraft firms during the expansion period ran without a hitch.

The delays encountered throughout the expansion programme undoubtedly caused the Air Council much worry, and in 1938 the Air Ministry began to apply some pressure and instructed the firms to expand production to the maximum physically possible, to establish night shifts, and to sub-contract at least a third of the work to outside firms. This may go some way to explaining the Air Council's very profound sense of frustration and disappointment with Supermarine since it had been known from the very earliest days that the company did not have the capacity to complete the Spitfire contract without sub-contracting, and that in many ways, therefore, the Spitfire was an experiment in production which the Air Council hoped would point the way to the rest of the industry. The delays and wrangles over the sub-contracting issue had therefore seriously jeopardized one of the major planks in the Air Ministry's long-term plan for aircraft production.

The Air Council's annoyance and frustration over Spitfire production delays is understandable when one considers the optimism of the early Supermarine forecasts in relation to the poor initial performance actually achieved. That the sub-contracting issue had been mishandled is not in doubt, but at the same time one might reasonably have asked where were the skilled and reliable sub-contractors to be found on the fringe of an industry which had been on starvation rations since 1919? Sudden increases in production capacity simultaneously with great forward strides in technology could not be switched on in emergency like an electric light. A lesson that might well be pondered in modern times.

The Air Council no doubt felt that Sir Robert McLean's early production forecasts had been blatant commercial gamesmanship. Be that as it may, it should not be forgotten that if Sir Robert had spelled out all the difficulties and pitfalls that would undoubtedly lie ahead, and had submitted cautious, conservative and coldly realistic estimates about Spitfire production prospects in 1936, it could well have resulted in the Spitfire's not being ordered at all, and that certainly would have been to nobody's

F.37/34 Final design for Prototype

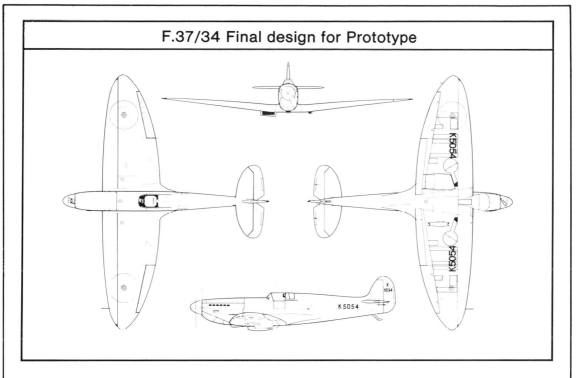

advantage except Germany's. Perhaps those early production traumas and the acrimonious disputes between McLean and the Air Council were, viewed in retrospect, a very small price to pay for the Spitfire and for the foundations of the massive production effort that was to follow.

CHAPTER 18

Death of R.J. Mitchell

In June 1937 — just one year after the placing of the production contract for the Spitfire — Supermarine suffered its most cruel and damaging blow in the death of R.J. Mitchell at the extraordinarily young age of forty-two.

He was in the twenty-second year of his service to the company and it is remarkable to look back upon what he achieved in that relatively short time.

Various R.J. Mitchell memorial lectures delivered to the Royal Aeronautical Society — notably that of Joseph Smith of 21 January 1954 — have listed the aircraft he designed and have dealt with some of the technical aspects of his work, and described the build-up of the design team which he created at Southampton which, apart from the Spitfire itself, was perhaps his most valuable and precious legacy to his country.

In 1933 R.J. had been operated on for cancer of the intestine. This operation was apparently successful and the doctors informed him that provided there was no recurrence of the trouble within four years his complete recovery could be assured.

But in early 1937, just four years later, the trouble recurred and it was decided in February 1937 that his best chance lay in a visit to the clinic in Vienna of Dr Anton Loew, then a world expert on Mitchell's form of cancer.

R.J. was flown out there in a chartered de Havilland Rapide which took off from Eastleigh aerodrome on a spring day in 1937. A large number of the Design Staff from Woolston somehow found it necessary to visit Eastleigh that morning and I well remember the scene as R.J.'s aeroplane taxied out in front of a crowd of his devoted staff who had assembled on the tarmac to wave him good luck and God speed. Alas, in spite of this tide of goodwill and high hopes, R.J. returned to England late in May with any last hope of recovery finally gone.

After the return from Vienna there was nothing for it but to await the end, which R.J. did with the utmost fortitude, putting his affairs in order from his home in Russell Place, Southampton.

He died on 11 June 1937.

Throughout the period during which R.J. inspired and led the design of the Spitfire he knew he was living in the shadow of death, but he did not flinch nor slacken his efforts. By the time the shadow became a reality in 1937 he had seen his prototype flying for more than a year and knew it was performing very much as he had hoped and intended. He knew also that it was ordered into production for the Royal Air Force and he had every reason to believe it would serve them and the country well.

As he lay dying at his home at Russell Place, which was quite close to the aerodrome, he would hear the sound of the Merlin engine as the Spitfire flew overhead and it is reasonable to suppose that he felt the satisfaction of knowing that yet another job had been well done. Just how well done, however, only the future would divulge.

R.J. flourished as a Chief Designer during the brave and formative years of aviation between the wars. Those were the days when the fortunes of an aircraft company depended very much upon the quality and character of its Chief Designer. No amount of management expertise nor capital investment could compensate for a bad or unsuccessful one. These were the days of the giants: men like Camm, Rex Pierson, Geoffrey de Havilland, Bishop, Barnwell, to mention a few. They were all very different, usually with widely differing backgrounds of training and experience and they faced very different problems.

The thing they had in common can best be defined as 'flair'. They exercised enormous influence upon the fortunes of their companies and upon the growth of an industry, and the security of a country.

As a breed they have tended to disappear due to the radically changed nature of the aircraft companies and the processes and technologies of design. But in their day they were the 'greats' and Reginald Joseph Mitchell was surely amongst the greatest.

One of Mitchell's longest-serving and, I think, most valued technical assistants, who became Head of the Supermarine Technical Office, was Alan Clifton, MBE, BSc(Eng), C.Eng, FRAES. Alan, whose personal contribution to Supermarine aircraft over the years and to the Spitfire in particular was enormous, wrote the following account of his early contacts with Supermarine and R.J. Mitchell:

On hearing from a friend at the Royal Aircraft Establishment that there was a vacancy for someone to do aircraft design calculations at the Supermarine Aircraft Works at Woolston, Southampton, I hastened to write to the firm asking for an interview the following Sunday and enclosing a postal order to pay for a reply by telegram. It came from R.J. Mitchell who, at the age of twenty-five, had been appointed Chief Engineer, and offered a meeting at his home in Woolston.

The meeting was quite informal and I received a letter dated 24th April 1923 offering 'a position on our staff at a salary of £3.10.0 per week for 6 months. At the end of this period your salary would be revised and adjusted according to how you had adapted yourself to the work and to what progress you had made in this period. We should like to point out that to anyone who is really keen on his work every opportunity will be given for advancement'.

I discovered later that Mitchell had advertised the job and got so many replies he ignored them, which emphasizes my good fortune.

Having completed an apprenticeship at a Staffordshire firm, Kerr Stuart and Company who built railway locomotives, Mitchell had joined Supermarine, or Pemberton Billing as it was then, in 1916. Very soon he was turning out comprehensive aircraft drawings. They bore no resemblance to the highly developed steam locomotive of his day.

It was in 1916 that Scott-Paine acquired the firm from Pemberton Billing and four years later promoted the youthful Mitchell to Chief Engineer and Designer, a tribute not only to Mitchell's outstanding ability but also to Scott-Paine's judgement. Among other things Mitchell was doing the design strength calculations which were then checked by the Royal Aircraft Establishment at Farnborough. He had acquired a prize for mathematics at the night school he attended during his apprenticeship and was thus academically competent; but it was his practical outlook and his drive which were outstanding. Although often highly experimental his racing aircraft were invariably tested and tried by the date of the race, though the order to proceed with detailed design and construction had been given barely six months previously.

His first *ab initio* design as Chief Engineer was for the 1920 Air Ministry competition for a commercial amphibian, in which the Supermarine aircraft took second place. But the second prize of £4,000 was doubled because in the opinion of the Air Ministry it was such an excellent design.

In 1922 the Sea Lion II flying boat, a modification of an existing design, won the Schneider Trophy, an international speed event. Mitchell's early designs were characterized by their practical and trouble-free nature. An example was the remarkable RAF Far Eastern Cruise by Southampton flying boats to Singapore, round Australia, up to Hong Kong and back to Singapore with the crews living on board. But there were also occasions when experimentation led to failure. In 1925 the startling S.4 twin-float monoplane broke with Supermarine traditional form and construction. Greatly admired for its beautiful clean lines, it would seem to have overstepped the bounds of current aeronautical knowledge for it crashed in Chesapeake Bay during the pre-race tests. Fortunately the firm's pilot, Henri Biard, survived. His close personal friendship with Mitchell was unaffected, and in fact Mitchell was always extremely concerned about pilot safety.

After the S.4 the S.5 (1927), the S.6 (1929) and the S.6B (1931) made a clean sweep of the bi-annual Schneider races. In this way Mitchell added to experience of reliable military aeroplanes the dimensions of drag and weight reduction in the extreme form for winning not merely Schneider races, but an absolute world speed record. It was during this period of less than ten years that construction was developed from the use mainly of wood to aluminium alloy.

In an article by Mitchell on 'Racing Seaplanes and Their Influence on Design' which appeared in the Aeronautical Engineering supplement to the *Aeroplane* dated 25 December 1929 the final sentence reads: '. . . and last (but no means least) the great value of close co-operation between engine and machine [i.e. airframe] designers'.

Thus was acquired a comprehensive range of design and manufacturing skills and practices appropriate to the most advanced aeronautical engineering.

In 1928 the firm was bought by Vickers and, with the object of capitalizing on these skills, a bid was put in and a prototype order obtained for a fighter landplane to A.M. specification F.7/30. The compromise which Mitchell struck between racing and military use was not judged good enough for production, but was sufficiently promising to lead to another prototype, a joint Rolls-Royce/Vickers Supermarine private venture.* Thus what became the famous Spitfire was conceived.

During the design phase Mitchell was recovering from an operation for cancer and knew the disease might recur. In the event it did recur and he died in 1937 at the age of forty-two knowing that the prototype had proved outstanding under Air Ministry tests and an initial production order had been placed with the firm.

There is no doubt however that Mitchell was extremely conscious of the menace of Hitler's Germany and although not in good health he put a tremendous effort into the Spitfire design.

During Mitchell's term as Chief Engineer a new design which was actually built† came out on average every ten months. This excludes modified forms and comprises a light aeroplane and a bomber as well as many amphibians and flying boats in addition to the Schneider planes and the fighters.

He would spend a lot of time in the drawing office silently cogitating on an individual detailed drawing, but accumulating a number of hangers-on who came to answer a question and stayed to learn. On such occasions Mitchell was tolerant of comment, some of it foolish or even provocative. He thought very deeply and Sir Henry Royce said of him: 'He had the ideal temperament for a designer — slow to decide and quick to act.' Known to all as 'R.J.', he gave credit where credit was due, and his relationship with his staff was devoid of 'stuffiness'.

On official occasions celebrating success, of which there were quite a few, he showed signs of shyness, but at the office Christmas dinner, for example, he was the life and soul of the party.

In his time technology was beginning to make itself felt, and he welcomed it, consulting top-ranking theorists. But theories had to pass the tests his common sense applied. As a draughtsman himself he respected the contribution made by individual members of the office. He was keen on sport, playing cricket and tennis, and learnt to pilot a Moth at the Hampshire Aeroplane Club during his last years. He took great pride in winning the prize in a landing competition.

---

*Eventually paid for by the Air Ministry.

†Two were cancelled when construction was well advanced.

With the benefit of hindsight I would describe him as a lovable character, pre-eminently practical, who had that infinite capacity of taking pains which is judged the hallmark of genius.

E.J. Davis worked with Mitchell as a senior draughtsman on the detail design for the prototype Spitfire. He wrote as follows:

> [Mitchell] was a thinker and spent hours alone in his office. However, he was an all-rounder and took interest in detail design. He would sit at a draughtsman's board surrounded by his entourage of senior men and make positive suggestions. He held strong views on some aspects of design. In particular he showed dislike of structures which, although having a high strength to weight ratio, failed by sudden collapse under test. He rejected these in favour of other types which gave advance signals of failure by slow deflections. He followed the jobs down to the workshops to inspect the finished products. On one occasion he picked up a rudder, decided it was too heavy and insisted, in no uncertain terms, on a redesign.

Another of R.J.'s early associates was Jock Rice, who has written as follows:

> I joined Supermarine in November 1922 as an engineering apprentice, and R.J. personally asked me, in February 1925, to join the then small design team to become specialized in electrics and radio (or 'wireless' as it then was). Of course it was all very fundamental in those days.
>
> The subject being a specialized one, I was in contact with R.J. frequently, and learnt to respect his honesty and clear thinking and, in particular, his clear-cut decision-making. But better than I can put it into words, and avoiding duplication, a reference to *Vickers: A History*, by J.D. Scott, page 200,* is all that is required!

The relevant paragraph from the above reference reads as follows:

> Mitchell was, in 1930, at the height of his powers as a designer. With a series of Schneider successes behind him he was confident of his own abilities — that peculiar mixture of hardheaded practicality and inventive dreaminess, the 'clear-thinking ability to create and notable capacity for leadership'* which made his methods as well as his achievements unforgettable. Though not lacking in temperament, Mitchell's nature was quiet and contemplative. On the other hand his genius was not a solitary one; he was a great listener . . .

These tributes, from men who knew him well and worked closely with him, speak more eloquently than any epitaph.

---

*J. Smith: Royal Aeronautical Society lecture.

Vickers: A History (Weidenfeld & Nicolson, 1962).

CHAPTER 19

Early Service

It is easy to forget, in the light of the impressive total of Spitfires eventually built, that the aircraft's long-term future was by no means assured even after deliveries to the squadrons had commenced. Indeed, it is quite plain that the Air Ministry did not appreciate the development potential of the aircraft, and that the Spitfire was regarded as only one stage in an ongoing process of fighter development. While in the spring of 1938, under the impetus provided by Scheme 'L', orders for 1,200 Spitfires had been placed with Supermarine (200) and the Nuffield organization (1,000), the Spitfire does not appear to have figured in the Air Staff's production plans much after 1940.

To understand why this was so it is necessary to have some insight into the RAF's thinking in regard to fighter aircraft at that time. The Spitfire and the Hurricane were both designed to a specification which was drawn up by the RAF in response to the rapid increases in speed being displayed by contemporary bomber aircraft. The Air Staff saw a need for swift, heavily armed fighters whose primary purpose was to be intercepting and shooting down bombers. These bombers, it was thought, would be fast and possibly armoured machines flying in formation, and speed and firepower would both be essential if any defending aircraft was to perform successfully against them. What the Air Staff did not foresee was that, when these bombers arrived over England in the summer of 1940, they were accompanied by fighter aircraft operating from newly captured bases in France and the Low Countries. Furthermore, many senior officers believed the day of the dog-fight to be past, a relic of a bygone era when aircraft flew slowly enough to allow pilots time to keep their sights on the target for longer than two seconds. The Spitfires and Hurricanes were to be bomber-destroyers, and at the time of their inception the single-seat multi-gun fighter was only one of several designs developed for this role: hence the Boulton Paul Defiant turret fighter, which proved so disappointing in combat. The Defiant, in point of fact, was not a failure in terms of its design philosophy, since it proved itself perfectly capable of shooting German bombers out of the sky. It was unable, however, to live in the same airspace as the higher performance single-seat fighters; the fault though lay in the philosophy, not the machine. It is a tribute to Mitchell and Camm that the Spitfire and Hurricane proved to be both efficient bomber-destroyers, and superlative fighters in the traditional sense, able to 'mix it' and survive.

In 1938, however, the Air Staff were still thinking in terms of the bomber-destroyer, and they were increasingly concerned about the possibility of the Germans' equipping the Luftwaffe's bombers with armour plate. It was therefore felt that a fighter aircraft armed with cannon, rather than machine-guns, was an urgent requirement. Thus, at a meeting of the Air Council on 26 July 1938 the Deputy Chief of the Air Staff, Air Vice-Marshal R. C. Peirse, whilst discussing the type of aircraft which should be ordered into production at the Fairey factory in Stockport, had some interesting comments to make on future fighter policy. 'DCAS said that the Royal Air Force was badly in need of a cannon fighter. Recent experiments carried out against a Blenheim showed that [for] machine-gun fire to be effective [it] must be intensive and prolonged. For this reason he thought it would be essential to introduce into the Service a cannon gun fighter in two or three years' time [i.e. 1940/1]. The Westland [Whirlwind] fighter could be equipped with either machine-guns or cannon guns. He would like to press very strongly that Faireys should build the Westland fighter.'

In the discussion which followed this statement the choice of aircraft for manufacture by Fairey was narrowed down to either Spitfires or Whirlwinds, and the very clear inference was that the Spitfire was considered to be approaching obsolescence. Indeed, in picking up on a statement by Sir Ernest Lemon that, if the Westland fighter proved a failure, 'it would be a mistake to give Fairey's an order for an obsolescent type of fighter when they had the design staff available to produce a better type', the Secretary of State for Air actually asked whether the Air Staff would regard the Spitfire as obsolescent by the time it could be put into production by Fairey. No straight answer was given, but it was stated that if Fairey could manufacture 310 Spitfires by March 1940 (i.e. as part of the present programme), 'it would be possible . . . to accept Spitfires': the implication was very clear: the Spitfire would be obsolescent by 1940.

At this point the story becomes inextricably enmeshed with the parallel expansion problems of the British aircraft industry. The headlong rush to expand the industry, with new factory space being erected and additional labour being taken on and trained as fast as possible, brought with it certain problems. Once factories were built or extended, and new workmen employed, they could not be left idle. It was therefore essential that the firms concerned be given aircraft orders to complete. New designs, however, could not be conjured out of a hat, and would in any case have to fit in with the RAF's long-term plans in order to avoid a multiplicity of types. To keep firms occupied and expanding whilst new types were designed it was necessary to place what were known as 'stop-gap' or 'gap-filler', orders for existing types. It was for this reason that so many of the obsolete types, such as the Fairey Battle, were eventually built.

It was expected that the Whirlwind would be capable of speeds of about 400 mph, and, with its heavy cannon armament, it would therefore represent a more efficient bomber-destroyer than the 350 mph machine-gun-armed Spitfire I. It was with these expectations in mind that, in December 1938, the Air Council began to consider orders for Supermarine once the current Spitfire con-

Early production Spitfire Is at Eastleigh. Quill centre figure.

tracts were completed in March 1940. Several production combinations were considered, including reducing the order for 1,000 Spitfires from Nuffield to 500, and substituting Whirlwinds, whilst giving Supermarine a further order for Spitfires to keep the factory in work. This further potential Spitfire order was thought of and referred to as a 'stop-gap' order (i.e. of a potentially obsolescent type) to keep the Supermarine workforce employed until production could be switched to Whirlwinds or a newer design. By the early part of 1939 consideration was being given to reducing Spitfire orders at Castle Bromwich in favour of heavy bombers, either Stirlings or Halifaxes.

The thinking behind all these plans and revisions is nicely illustrated by the following exchanges which took place at a meeting in July 1939. 'ADMP [Sir Wilfrid Freeman] said that the delay in the production of the new types involved a replanning for the production of those types within a shorter period, if the RAF re-equipment programme was not to be delayed. This concentration in production would in turn involve building up a much larger trained labour force . . . To train and progressively build up the labour force to permit the maximum production attainable on current types during the next eighteen months and the concentration of the production on new types, it would be necessary to give stop-gap orders for current types amounting to approximately 2,000 aircraft.'

Spitfires were then specifically mentioned in this context, together with several other aircraft types, and it was further stated that 'these aircraft [types] would be of genuine value for war purposes during 1940, but would not continue to have such value after 1940'. Freeman had earlier minuted the Chief of the Air Staff suggesting that Supermarine be given a 'gap-filling' contract for 100 Spitfires to take the firm through to September 1940, when a new aircraft could be put into production (Freeman favoured either the Beaufighter or a Gloster design) and any surplus Spitfires over and above those required under the expansion schemes could be released for sale to foreign customers.

The Spitfire was to continue in production because several factors combined to alter the Air Council's perception of the problem. Firstly, of course, and perhaps most importantly in the short term, war loomed ever closer, and the storm finally broke in September 1939. Orders for a further 450 Spitfires were placed in August 1939 and March 1940. Of more importance in the long term were the serious problems and delays encountered with the proposed successors to the Spitfire and Hurricane. The Westland Whirlwind was beset by various teething problems and difficulties with its Rolls-Royce Peregrine engines, which meant that the first production aircraft were not delivered until June 1940. Although the engine problems were overcome in suadron service, having a speed of 360 mph at 15,000 ft., and poor performance at altitude, the Whirlwind offered few advantages over the Spitfire and only 112 were built.

Hawkers, meanwhile, had been busy working on designs for a single-engined Hurricane/Spitfire replacement under Specification F.18/37. Two prototypes were built, one powered by the Rolls-Royce Vulture and the other by the Napier Sabre, and they became, respectively, the Hawker Tornado and the Hawker Typhoon. The Hawker Tornado, a large, robust, and heavily armed fighter made its firsts flight in 1940. This was regarded by the Air Staff as their Spitfire replacement of 1941–2, and 1,000 aircraft had been ordered to be built at Avro, Manchester. The problems with the Vulture engine — an 'X' layout which was virtually two Kestrels mounted on a common crankcase — led however to its abandonment, which brought the Tornado programme to a standstill. The Vulture engine, incidentally, also powered the Manchester twin-engined bomber which was subsequently re-engined with four Merlins, thus producing the most successful bomber of the war, the Lancaster. The Napier Sabre also suffered from severe teething problems and the Typhoon did not enter service until September 1941.

These difficulties in the Hawker and Westland programmes meant that the RAF faced the prospect of soldiering on through 1940 and into 1941 without a modern cannon-armed interceptor fighter, and in consequence the Air Ministry began to consider the fitting of cannons into Spitfires and Hurricanes. This had not previously been thought an attractive proposition, as the French Hispano 20mm cannon selected for the RAF generated greater recoil forces than the .303 Browning, and therefore required a more rigid mounting. In twin-engined designs, such as the Whirlwind and the Beaufighter, the cannon armament could be mounted rigidly in the nose, but the Air Ministry entertained very real doubt concerning the degree of rigidity which it would be

Spitfire Is of 19 Sqn. flying from Duxford

possible to attain in an installation in the wing of a small fighter. Indeed, one member of the Operational Requirements Branch stated in a minute in June 1938; 'In my opinion wing-mounted cannon are likely to give us all sorts of trouble.' These fears were possibly exaggerated, but by no means entirely groundless, as the early problems with the rigidity of the cannon installations in the Mark IB showed. See Chapter 21.)

The failure to produce a viable successor in the required time-scale joined with the exigencies of the war to give the Spitfire a new lease of life. The combined efforts of Joseph Smith and Rolls-Royce in producing increasing amounts of power from the Merlin, and then successfully fitting the improved versions and the heavier armament into the airframe, together with the un-doubted success of the Spitfire in combat, particularly at Dunkirk (see Chapter 22), convinced the Air Staff that the aircraft should continue in production.

It should perhaps be made plain that the Air Staff were quite correct in planning to replace the Spitfire. Their expectation that newer designs would prove superior was not unreasonable, nor was their estimate that the Mark I would prove obsolescent by the end of 1940 incorrect. The remarkable development potential of the Spitfire, however, confounded all these estimates. It was as well that it did, since both the Whirlwind and the Typhoon proved to be markedly inferior aircraft at high altitude.

Night flying trials at East-leigh of the prototype in the glare of floodlights

It is doubtful if these questions of high policy and production percolated down to the pilots of 19 and 66 Squadrons, who were, in the last months of 1938, busily engaged in trying to master the new breed of fighter with its racy lines, and unfamiliar features such as enclosed cockpit and retracting undercarriage. During 1939 they were joined by increasing numbers of RAF fighter squadrons, including the first of the Auxiliary Air Force squadrons, No 602 (City of Glasgow), who were soon to achieve an unusual distinction (see page 108). Inevitably, as with the introduction into service of any new aircraft, there were teething problems, and prominent among them was the fallibility of the human memory. Royal Air Force pilots at that time were still unfamiliar with the idea of the retractable undercarriage, and a spate of incidents occurred where the pilot forgot to lower the wheels before alighting on the aerodrome.

Two such instances must have been particularly embarrassing in this regard: an officer of 602 Squadron was landing in formation, and used his radio to warn his colleague that he had not lowered his undercarriage; in doing so he completely forgot to lower his own! And one Sergeant J.A. Potter of 19 Squadron suffered a more public humiliation when he made a wheels up landing during the spot-landing competition at the Empire Air Day display at Duxford in 1938. He was fined five pounds, a considerable sum for those days. The Spitfire was fitted with a

Spitfire Is of 609 Sqn. 1940

warning horn designed to operate at a certain airspeed to alert the pilot to the fact that the undercarriage was still in the raised position. The horn tended to sound at too high an airspeed, however, and pilots often turned it off altogether, or became so used to the sound that they failed to register its significance.

There were also several accidents during night flying practice; the Spitfire at this stage being considered suitable for both day and night fighting. The restricted forward vision over the long nose, and problems with the glare from the Merlin's stub exhausts, necessitated a long curving approach and good judgement of height, airspeed and attitude. The narrow-track undercarriage and poorly lit airfields were unforgiving of an error in this regard. Pilots also displayed a tendency to misjudge the Spitfire's angle of descent and undershoot the airfield, a fault compounded by early problems with the oiling up of windscreens. In general, though, the viceless qualities of the aircraft made its transition into service relatively trouble-free.

By the outbreak of war on 3 September 1939 there were nine operational Spitfire squadrons, with exactly 150 serviceable Spitfires out of a total strength of 171 aircraft (88%).* The Air

---

*These figures do not include No. 609 Squadron which was re-equipping with Spitfires, but was not yet operational.

Staff and fighter pilots waited expectantly for the Luftwaffe to deliver the predicted 'knock-out blow'; it never materialized. Instead the Spitfire had to wait for more than a month before it fired its guns in anger for the first time on 16 October. On that day aircraft from 602 and 603 Squadrons, the two rival Scottish auxiliary units, intercepted an air raid on the Royal Navy's anchorage in the Firth of Forth. Three aircraft of 'B' Flight 602 Squadron shot down a German aircraft, probably a Ju 88, into the sea 45 miles north of St Abbs Head. At almost the same moment three Spitfires of 603 squadron shot down a further bomber off Port Seton. The first 'kill' by a Royal Air Force fighter was officially credited to a Spitfire of 603 Squadron, but the comparative times of destruction of the two aircraft were so close as to make distinction invidious.

On 28 October the same two squadrons brought down a Heinkel 111 of Kampfgeschwader 26. The Heinkel had taken off from the Isle of Sylt on an armed reconnaissance mission over the Firth of Forth, but bursting anti-aircraft shells from Royal Navy ships in the estuary had attracted the patrolling fighters from 602 and 603 Squadrons and a section of Spitfires from each unit attacked the bomber. With one engine out of action and two of the crew dead the German pilot crash-landed the aircraft near the village of Humbie; the first German aircraft to be brought down on British soil during the Second World War. It is altogether fitting that these early victories, the first of many gained by Fighter Command during the course of the war, should have fallen to the Spitfire, the only Allied fighter to see operational service from the first day of the war to the last.

This was a pattern the Hurricane and Spitfire squadrons of Fighter Command were to become familiar with over the next six months, as they pursued elusive German reconnaissance aircraft and isolated raiders. The absence of any whole-hearted attack from the Luftwaffe, and the war's general air of lethargy and unreality, led to the coining of the phrase the 'phoney war'. It was not to remain phoney for very long.

CHAPTER 20

The Succession

The death of R.J. Mitchell at once created an urgent and difficult problem of succession. An organization such as the Design Department which Mitchell had created at Supermarine could not be left leaderless for even the shortest period and at the time that he died it was in any case under great and unusual pressure due to the problems that were arising in getting the Spitfire into production.

Mitchell had had a technical assistant in the person of Major H.J. Payn AFC, RAF(ret), known to everybody as 'Agony' Payn, who had been a distinguished fighter pilot in World War I and had served in No. 56 Squadron under the famous Major James McCudden VC, DSO, MC. He is, in fact, mentioned in some of McCudden's combat reports. He retired from the RAF in 1924 and was engaged by Vickers. He was well qualified technically, so as an immediate action Sir Robert McLean appointed Payn as Manager of the Design Department, and he appointed Rex Pierson (the Chief Designer at Weybridge who enjoyed great prestige and standing within the industry and also within the Air Ministry) to a position of overall supervisory control over the Supermarine Design Team which he would exercise by making regular and frequent visits.

It is not certain whether McLean intended this to be a purely temporary arrangement while he cast around for a suitable replacement for R.J. as Chief Designer at Supermarine, or whether he had in mind the eventual integration of the two design departments under a single Chief Designer. In my view he was unlikely to have adopted the second solution because the Supermarine Design Department, as created by Mitchell, had a very individual character of its own and the skills and specializations it had developed over the the years were different from those developed at Weybridge. The integration of the two departments would therefore have been difficult and almost certainly damaging, especially at a moment when both were under extreme pressure.

However, events were to intervene in so far that Payn had recently married a lady of foreign origin who was regarded by the authorities as a bad security risk, and in these circumstances he could no longer retain his senior position in the Supermarine design organization and had to leave.

This interlude had no doubt provided time and opportunity for more mature consideration of the problem and McLean appointed Joseph Smith as Manager of the Design Department, still under the Supervisory control of Rex Pierson, but later raised

Joseph Smith took over as Chief Designer at Supermarine upon the untimely death of R. J. Mitchell in 1937. He led the team which developed the Spitfire and its immediate successors into the transonic age

to the position of Chief Designer, thus restoring the Department to the state of independence and autonomy it had enjoyed under the guidance of R.J. Mitchell.

In Mitchell's day Joe Smith had held the important senior post of Chief Draughtsman and as such had really created over the years the Drawing Office at Woolston which had grown from very small beginnings. It was in the Drawing Office that all the detail design was done once the main lines, dimensions and numerous other parameters of a new project were settled, and it was from the drawing office (always known as the D.O.) that the final working drawings were made for issue to the shops.

Therefore the detail design of the Spitfire had been done in the Drawing Office and as has been previously mentioned the structural design was technologically very advanced for its day.

Joe Smith would have had a great deal to do with it and he

therefore stepped into the arduous and responsible job of Chief Designer armed with a deep, extensive, and detailed knowledge of the Spitfire design in most of its aspects; above all he had acquired over the years an intimate knowledge and understanding of how R.J.'s mind worked.

Joe often used to describe from his memories of his days as Chief Draughtsman R.J.'s practice of periodically making a tour of the drawing-boards and poring over a drawing with great care and closely questioning the draughtsman who had prepared it. In the course of these visits and discussions at the various boards he would usually gather a train of followers comprising senior technicians or other draughtsmen and anyone else who felt they could get away with attaching themselves to the bandwagon. All would listen carefully to the great man's comments. This was one of the ways in which R.J. spread his ideas and general philo-sophies throughout the design organization. His comments were sometimes fiercely critical but always constructive. He would usually have in his pocket a stub of thick, soft pencil, probably about 2B, and he had a great eye for line (which is, I suppose, self-evident) and often he would produce his stub of pencil and, leaning over the board, would modify an outline freehand. As Joe remarked, R.J.'s freehand lines were often about 3/8 in thick, but by carefully establishing the mean centre a modified drawing which satisfied him could usually be produced.

Joe Smith had served his engineering apprenticeship at the Austin Motor Company in Birmingham. He joined the Super-marine Company as a senior draughtsman in 1921 and became Chief Draughtsman in 1926, so he had some sixteen years of experience of working closely with R.J.

Joe Smith was a very practical man with a direct and fairly uncomplicated approach to most problems. It is perhaps para-doxical to describe a distinguished aircraft engineer as a man with both feet firmly on the ground but this is the best way to describe him.

Fate brought him into the job in 1937 at a moment of peculiar significance. Hitler's lowering threat to the safety of Europe and the free world was now apparent to all but the blindest. R.J.'s creative genius had produced the Spitfire; Henry Royce and Ernest Hives had inspired the creation of the Merlin engine; it now remained to give practical effect to the development and production of a weapon which the situation so urgently deman-ded. The difficulties lying ahead were enormous.

It is remarkable in retrospect how much depended at that time upon the performance of relatively few men in the industry, in the Government, in the Air Ministry and the Air Force. Joe Smith was destined to be one of the very key men.

Before Mitchell died he had almost completed the design of a new heavy bomber to Air Ministry specification B12/36 which was to have four Merlin engines. The predicted performance of this aircraft was spectacular and it had been ordered in prototype form. The first prototype was in an advanced stage of building at the Woolston Works when it was destroyed in a German bombing raid in September 1940. Probably the Germans never knew how much they had achieved in that raid for whilst it caused only a temporary interruption to Spitfire production it finished the Supermarine B12/36 for ever.

But for this Mitchell might have finished up as the man who not only designed the best British fighter of World War II but the best British bomber also. Had the B12/36 not been destroyed in 1940 before it flew it could have exacted a terrible penalty upon Hitler's Germany in the later stages of the war. So when Joe took over the job in 1937 the detail design task of the B12/36 bomber was an additional commitment at Supermarine.

This is mentioned to make the point that before his untimely death in 1937 R.J. was already in the business of conquering fresh fields and most of the design load involved in getting the Spitfire into production would have descended upon Joe Smith's shoulders anyway. In spite of the traumas experienced between 1936 and 1938 (See Chapter 17) in productionizing the Spitfire Smith's shoulders were broad enough to take the load, albeit with some delay, and later to mastermind the remarkable development of the Spitfire in performance, fighting capability and role application throughout the war.

Joe was a man of great character and determination. He was tough, did not suffer fools gladly and was impatient of idleness or shoddy work. He inspired a genuine liking and respect amongst those who worked for him. He was a worthy, and perhaps in the dramatically changing circumstances of the time, the only possible successor to R.J.

CHAPTER 21

Development

'If Mitchell was born to design the "Spitfire"' wrote J.D. Scott,*
'Joe Smith was born to defend and develop it.'

Because of the difficulties and delays in getting the aeroplane
into production, and the bad relations which developed between
the Air Council and Supermarine, the Spitfire can be said to have
got off to a bad and controversial start which could seriously have
damaged its prospects. Its chief asset — its superior performance
in speed and climb — was not then perhaps regarded as necessari-
ly a decisive factor in its favour. Both Hurricane and Spitfire were
regarded by the Air Staff as bomber-destroyers. The threat was
perceived to be attacks by massed formations of enemy bomber
aircraft. The main requirement was therefore to have enough
fighters capable of catching and intercepting them and of in-
flicting an unacceptable attrition rate upon them.

A critically important advance had been made in fighter armament which applied equally to Hurricane and Spitfire, but more
would no doubt be required in the future. Thoughts had already
turned towards heavy-calibre cannon and progress in this direction had been made in France.

Numbers could be the name of the game when talking of
fighters, which already had a comfortable 100-mph advantage
over modern bombers anyway. So availability, ease of rapid
production, reliability and ease of maintenance in service and,
above all, cost were the dominant factors.

The command and control system based on a chain of RDF
(radar) stations and a complex communication system was still in
an early stage of development and there was no certainty that
such an esoteric concept would really be effective. So the air
defence of the country might well depend simply upon having
enough fighters with enough performance rather than having
some of them with a performance like a Schneider racer.

The Spitfire's best friends when it first entered service were the
young fighter pilots of the Royal Air Force. It has been truly said
that it was 'a pilot's aeroplane'. From the moment you entered the
cockpit it felt right and you felt comfortable and confident. The
cockpit was small, neat and well laid out, and the pilot had a sense
of sitting in just the right place, not too far forward and not too far
back, not too high and not too low. Ahead stretched the long sleek
nose containing the powerful Merlin engine, and although this
obscured a good deal of forward view on the ground nevertheless

---

Vickers: A History, Weidenfeld & Nicolson, 1962.

on a breed of young men much addicted to fast sports cars it had precisely the right impact.

Before flying the Spitfire most pilots' previous experience had been on very much lower performance aircraft, either trainers such as the Miles Master or the snub-nosed, radial-engined biplane fighters of an earlier vintage. By comparison the Spitfire seemed to slip through the air at speeds much higher than the pilots had ever experienced before and with a sort of casual ease. Again, by comparison with previous experience, it handled beautifully in the air and its liveliness imparted a sense of challenge. There was just the right feeling of having a tiger by the tail.

Everybody wanted to fly a Spitfire and from the young men in the early Spitfire squadrons a tide of enthusiasm and excitement came welling upwards which clearly found its way to the Command levels. But certainly time would be needed for the Spitfire to achieve full acceptance within the Royal Air Force, particularly among the senior ranks, and this was the situation soon after Joe Smith found himself responsible for all design aspects at Supermarine.

Since 1936 a number of design studies of more advanced fighters had been carried out at Supermarine. There had been a design for a two-seater turret fighter (looking surprisingly like the Spitfire), and another of a twin-engined, multi-gun fighter with its heavy armament packed into the nose of the fuselage; but none of these were developed into prototype form.

At some point, either before or after the outbreak of war, Joe Smith and his immediate technical advisers had reached the conclusion that Mitchell's design of the Spitfire had a potential for performance growth as well as for development in other directions, such as in the provision of heavier armament, which clearly suggested a policy of progressive development rather than dalliance with new designs. Such had been the problems of establishing the Spitfire in quantity production and such was the urgency of the military situation that a repetition of these problems could not be contemplated. Clearly the future would depend heavily upon a steady and progressive power-growth being achieved by Rolls-Royce with the Merlin engine and there was a growing confidence in this. In 1937 we flew at Supermarine a special Spitfire N.17, ordered by the Air Ministry, which was intended to attack the then world speed record, held by Germany.

It had reduced wing area and some drag-reducing requirements, but in particular it had a 'sprint' or 'Schneiderised' Merlin engine developed to give no less than 2,000 hp for a short period running on a special fuel mixture devised by Rod Banks of the Associated Ethyl Company, the man who had produced the fuel for the 'R' Type engine in the S.6B, and previous Schneider contestants.

Bench-testing of the special Merlin took place at Derby between August 1937 and May 1938, and more than 2,000 hp was recorded. This greatly increased power was obtained by running the engine completely unthrottled, thus using the full capacity of the supercharger at sea level, at 3,200 rpm (as against the normal

The High Speed Spitfire. The 48th production Mk I was converted and cleaned up to attempt to beat the World Air Speed Record. It had a special Merlin III engine delivering 2,160 hp but, although it recorded 410 mph, cooling problems caused the attempt to be abandoned in 1939

3,000), which produced the remarkable manifold or 'boost' pressure of plus 27½lb. Special spark plugs were needed which had to be fitted after the engine had been started and warmed up on the ground. I was flying this aircraft at Eastleigh between December 1938 and March 1939 and although we did not achieve enough speed to attack the world speed record, which had in the meantime been increased to 469.22 mph by the Germans, the fact was that in 1938 I was running that Merlin engine at a power output of 2,000 hp, double its normal power, and we achieved a speed of 408 mph at sea level (almost identical to the S.6B's speed record). This was not fast enough to take the record so we then embarked upon some fundamental changes to the cooling system designed to reduce the cooling drag, but before we were able to fly this the war intervened and N.17 was reverted to something like its normal configuration and given the PRU for use as a hack aircraft.

This abortive attempt on the world speed record was of minor importance in the context of world events and had been embarked upon primarily for propaganda reasons. Of immense importance, however, was that in 1938–9 we were running a Merlin engine at Southampton at a power output of 2,000 hp. True, it was a racing engine, operating for strictly limited periods under essentially sprint conditions with special fuel, special plugs and special starting procedures, but nevertheless there was 2,000 hp coming from a Merlin for all to see in 1939.

This had a powerful practical effect in convincing Joe Smith and his team at Supermarine of the power-growth which might reasonably be expected from the Merlin engine during the ensuing years, and so was an important factor in persuading Supermarine that the right policy for the firm lay in the continued development of Mitchell's Spitfire design which would proceed hand-in-hand with the power-growth of the Merlin at Rolls-Royce.

Thus, while the Supermarine design team were steadily becoming more convinced of the potential of the Spitfire the demise of the Tornado, and the setbacks and disappointments experienced with the Typhoon and Whirlwind created a serious gap in the Air Staff's future plans.

The Merlin production shop at Derby

Then, as is described in Chapter 22, the operations at Dunkirk revealed the critical importance of the Spitfire's extra performance and in particular its advantage in turning manoeuvre. Thus a series of converging events combined to create a situation whereby there was no available alternative, by the end of the Battle of Britain, but to carry on with the Spitfire and the Merlin and to develop both to the maximum of their potential and to build upon the extensive production base which had been created at Supermarine and Castle Bromwich, and Rolls-Royce at Derby, Crewe and Glasgow. Thus, not for the first or last time in the history of aviation, the right answer was found for the wrong (or at least fortuitous) reasons.

However, if the Spitfire was to go on where others had failed the incorporation of heavy-calibre cannon armament would be absolutely essential and this was one of the first development problems which Joe Smith and his design department had to cope with.

The Hispano-Suiza 20mm cannon was the chosen gun, and arrangements had been made for its production in this country. The problems of installation were great. The Spitfire wing was very thin (the difficulty in fitting eight machine-guns rather than four has already been discussed). Now here was a requirement to

A Merlin repair shop at Derby in World War II

fit much larger guns, firing larger, heavier and more ammunition with much greater recoil forces to be accommodated by the wing structure.

Within the Air Staff there were considerable doubts as to whether there would be enough rigidity in the wing of a small fighter such as the Spitfire to meet the case.

A Spitfire fitted with two cannon was produced for service trials in December 1939, and 30 Mk. IBs fitted with two cannon and four machine-guns were delivered to No. 19 Squadron at Duxford in August 1940. These early cannon installations had a drum-feed arrangement which was unsatisfactory and caused constant stoppages, but eventually a belt-feed system was developed, and this was satisfactory.

The first series production Spitfires to enter squadron service, fitted with two 20mm Hispano-Suiza cannon (one in each wing), plus two .303 machine-guns in each wing, was the Mk.VB, which entered squadron service in 1941. From that point onwards every Spitfire produced was cannon-armed, and the later Marks carried four.

The next design development task to be tackled by Joe Smith was the installation in a Spitfire of the larger, heavier and more powerful Griffon engine.

Shortly before the outbreak of war Rolls-Royce had decided to resurrect the old 'R' Type racing engine in production form, as a military engine. This was partly because they foresaw an early need for an engine of basically greater power at low level for the Fleet Air Arm for carrier operation and partly because they foresaw that sooner or later the Merlin might reach the limit of its power-growth potential and therefore an engine of greater cubic capacity should be, as it were, waiting in the wings. Hives used the phrase 'a second power string for the Spitfire'. It was to be called the Griffon, thus once again following the long-established Rolls-Royce practice of naming their engines after birds of prey.

It was during 1939, before the war started, that Joe Smith began to tackle the problem of what some people thought would not be possible: to fit the longer and heavier 37-litre Griffon engine within the slender lines of the Spitfire; and work started on the project in 1939.

Fortunately, as the old 'R' Type engine had been designed for racing, the lowest possible frontal area had been a paramount design requirement and the Griffon had a frontal area of only 7.9 sq. ft as against the 7.5 sq. ft of the Merlin, which was a very small increase in return for an extra 10 litres of cylinder capacity.

Smith's design for a Griffon-engined Spitfire was submitted to the Air Ministry in Supermarine's specification N. 466 in October 1939 and it received the immediate support and encouragement both of Air Marshal Sir Wilfrid Freeman (AMDP) and Mr N.E. Rowe, the Director of Technical Development.

This in itself is significant because it suggests that Sir Wilfrid Freeman, a man whose eyes were very definitely equipped with long-distance and wide-angle lenses, was by that time aware that the Spitfire might have to be developed to a much more advanced stage in the future and he no doubt saw provision for the Griffon engine as a prudent form of insurance.

The first Spitfire powered with a Griffon engine, DP 845 fitted with the RG.2SM, made its first flight in the hands of the author, at Worthy Down in November 1941. With later developments of the Griffon this led on to the Mks. XII and XIV, Seafires Mks. 15 and 17, and Spitfires Mks. 21, 22 and 24.

Thus two major and fundamental steps in the process of development of the Spitfire — the provision of cannon armament and provision for the future use of the Griffon engine — were both taken in the early years of Joe Smith's 'reign' as Chief Designer at Supermarine.

As explained in the Preface, this Book makes no claim to be a history of the Spitfire. If it did a very large proportion of the story would be devoted to the remarkable manner in which the Spitfire was developed and improved during the war both in perform-ance, and in its capacity to undertake important military roles which were never even considered at the time of Mitchell's original design such, for instance, as its use as a carrier-borne naval fighter and a high-performance strategic reconnaissance system. No fewer than fifty-two operational variants were pro-duced and went into operational service (see Appendix 4). Some of these were, of course, very minor variants embodying small changes in armament, equipment, or engine specification, but nevertheless requiring a change in designation. Others were major design changes involving large increments in performance and general operational capability such as those which accom-panied the introduction of the Mks. IX and VIII, the Mks. XII

Leonard G. Gooch, whose masterly forward planning enabled Spitfire production to be restarted quickly after the Supermarine works were bombed in 1940

and XIV, and ultimately the Mks. 21, 22 and 24 (which came out too late to play an operational role in the war). Most of these major forward strides generated equivalents in the photo-reconnaissance field and in the carrier-borne equivalents, the Seafires.

Two major forward strides in the performance of the Spitfire occurred between the Battle of Britain and the end of the war. These can best be described as the quantum jumps. They were the introduction of the Mk. IX with the Merlin 61 engine in 1942, and the Mk. XIV with the Griffon 65 engine in 1943. Diagrams of these two dramatic performance jumps appear on page 134.

The fact that the Spitfire had this potential is perhaps the best tribute to the soundness of R.J. Mitchell's original design which was then exploited, after his death, by the team of Supermarine designers operating under Joseph Smith's leadership and with the essential backing of the Rolls-Royce achievement over the years in the way of engine power-growth.

Mitchell bequeathed to his country two legacies of incalculable value: the Spitfire itself, and the team of designers which he had built up over the years and which could therefore carry on his work.

The achievements of Supermarine's design team in developing the Spitfire have perhaps not been emphasized as they should have been. The design organization expanded rapidly in size and scope from 1937 onwards.

After the bombing of the Woolston Works in September 1940 the Department was hurriedly evacuated to Southampton University as an immediate measure, and then a large country house, Hursley Park near Winchester, was taken over. Here a big drawing office was built in the grounds and other facilities were established, including an experimental shop which was thus located with easy accessibility to the drawing office.

The senior management of the company was also located at Hursley Park, which thus became the nerve centre of the Supermarine organization, including the production dispersion scheme.

It is not possible to mention the names individually of the many designers who made such a great contribution to the extraordinary development process achieved with the Spitfire between 1938 and 1945. One man, however, must be mentioned: Alan N. Clifton, MBE, B.Sc(Eng), C.Eng, FRAeS. He was engaged by R.J. Mitchell in 1923 to 'do aircraft design calculations'. He soon became Mitchell's principal technical assistant, a position which he held throughout the war. Thus he served as head of the Technical Office under both Mitchell and Joe Smith. Alan Clifton's contribution to the Supermarine design effort in the pre-Spitfire days was very significant; his contribution to the Spitfire itself is immeasurable.

To Joseph Smith must go the honour and credit for having inspired and led this team in the vital second phase in the design effort.

Pilots of 303 Polish (F) Sqn. with the fin of a Junkers Ju88, the 178th Enemy aircraft to be destroyed by the Squadran

CHAPTER 22

The Air Battles over Dunkirk

The 'phoney war' ended abruptly with the German invasion of France and the Low Countries on 10 May 1940. In accordance with their pre-prepared plans British and French armies moved across the border into Belgium and advanced to the River Dyle in an attempt to prevent the Germans occupying the Low Countries and outflanking the Maginot Line. Hurricanes of the BEF's Air Component provided air cover for this advance, whilst aircraft from Fighter Command patrolled along the Belgian and Dutch coasts to protect the Army's flank. It was on the 12 May, during one of these coastal patrols, that Spitfires first patrolled across the Channel;* until that date Dowding had jealously husbanded his reserves of what he considered his best aircraft.

Over the next two weeks Fighter Command's Spitfire squadrons were called upon to provide increasing numbers of aircraft for these patrols, an ominous sign of the heavy demands being placed on the Hurricane squadrons by Continental commitments. On the ground the Wehrmacht had pierced the Allied front opposite the Ardennes, and, moving at terrific speed, had succeeded in cutting off the British and French armies in Belgium from the bulk of the French forces in France. The BEF and a large proportion of the French forces fell back, in reasonably good order, to the Channel coast, where the hastily arranged evacuation plan. Operation Dynamo,, started on 26 May, although many civilians and non-fighting troops had already been taken off before that date.

Fighter Command was tasked with providing air cover for the evacuation and it was thus that the Spitfire was first involved in a large-scale aerial battle with a significant portion of the Luftwaffe. Many of the squadron pilots, however, were never aware that the BEF was fighting for its very existence below them, and indeed so far as many of them were concerned the aerial fighting during May was all part of one battle which became more intensive at the end of the month. Intensive being very definitely a relative term, since between 10 and 25 May 1940 Fighter Command had lost 82 aircraft, including 20 Spitfires and 50 or so Hurricanes, and 11 Group, whose commander, Air Vice-Marshal Keith Park, was to be responsible for directing the battle over Dunkirk, had already lost 54 pilots killed or missing. Nor were casualties to aircraft and pilots Park's only problems: he had only 16 squadrons available to

---

*Photo-reconnaissance Spitfires had been flying over the Continent for some time.

him, perhaps some 190 to 200 aircraft in all if serviceability rates were high, and only a limited number of airfields in Kent and Essex within operational range of Dunkirk. No 11 Group's Hurricanes and Spitfires were thus restricted in the amount of time they were able to spend over the Continent; the absolute maximum being forty minutes if flying from Manston or Hawkinge.

Park's orders from the Air Ministry were to provide continuous cover during the hours of daylight, and, in consequence of the limitations outlined above, he was forced to fly off weak patrols at regular intervals throughout the day from dawn to dusk. The Air Ministry's Official Narrative of the fighting gives a succinct summation of the problem: 'It will be seen that Fighter Command was required to meet, so far as was practicable with the available forces and bases, two virtually conflicting requirements over Dunkirk, continuity and strength.' Continuity, because the Air Ministry was under pressure from the Admiralty and the War Office to provide constant cover, and strength, because the German formations which appeared over Dunkirk could be expected to be large and well escorted, and could not be countered effectively by numerically weak RAF formations. For the first two days of the fighting, however, this was exactly what happened. Hamstrung by Air Ministry orders for a constant presence, Fighter Command patrolled at only squadron strength with mixed success. On the 27th: 'These patrols frequently encountered hostile forces throughout the day — in general of a size permitting of combat on not too unequal terms, but on occasion so large that our fighters were considerably outnumbered.' The RAF squadrons, in patrols as weak as nine aircraft, and at no time more than twenty strong, could not prevent the Luftwaffe bombers from severely damaging the port facilities and laying waste to Dunkirk town. The pall of smoke which hung over

Dunkirk throughout the evacuation served as a useful navigation mark for many of the RAF pilots, however.

Park repeatedly badgered the Air Ministry, through Dowding, and eventually secured a relaxation in the Ministry's former insistence on a permanent presence over the beaches, and from 29 May Park was permitted to exercise his 'discretion' in achieving his objective. Accepting the risks of longer gaps between patrols, he dispatched patrols three or four squadrons strong. This had been made doubly necessary since the Germans had begun to make increasing use of strong fighter formations moving in ahead of the bombers with the obvious intention of neutralizing any Fighter Command forces on patrol over the beaches. Most of the combats on this day took place between the opposing fighters, and the German bombers were able to sink at least eight ships whilst the RAF fighters fought with their escorts.

For the remainder of Operation Dynamo Fighter Command continued to operate on this pattern with varying degrees of success. In general the RAF's patrols successfully prevented the Germans achieving air superiority over Dunkirk and thus, with some assistance from the weather, considerably reduced the effectiveness of the bombing. Nevertheless the Luftwaffe aircrews were skilful and tenacious opponents, and by exploiting the gaps betweeen the RAF fighter patrols, or drawing them into combat with the escort, the Germans were able to exact a heavy toll in both lives and shipping. Their success in sinking 10 ships and damaging a further 12 on 1 June brought a reluctant decision to confine the evacuation to the hours of darkness. As far as the air operations were concerned this eased 11 Group's burden considerably, as they were now able to concentrate their patrols at dawn and dusk, when shipping was leaving or approaching the port. But it also reduced the number of men who could be rescued on any one day, and after 4 June attempts to evacuate the considerable numbers of French troops still in Dunkirk were abandoned.

At the time it was thought that the RAF had won a major victory over the much-vaunted Luftwaffe, with squadrons claiming 262 German aircraft definitely destroyed. Post-war analysis of captured German documents showed that these claims, made in good faith after the stress and confusion of battle, were considerably exaggerated. It may be, in fact that, on a strictly numerical index of losses, Fighter Command suffered something of a setback in the air-to-air combat over Dunkirk, since a total of 98 single-engined fighters, including 46 Spitfires, were lost, whereas Luftwaffe losses were in the region of 130 aircraft, a proportion of which undoubtedly fell to anti-aircraft fire and non-Fighter Command aircraft. Nevertheless, the RAF pilots were convinced that they had come out on top and their morale was correspondingly heightened. It is as well that the exaggerated claims were accepted as fact, since the pilots' belief that they were as good as, or better than, the enemy, was to sustain them through the difficult days of the Battle of Britain. They had, in truth, achieved much by preventing the Luftwaffe achieving its primary aim, which was to halt the evacuation and destroy the BEF.

There were, of course, many other factors which contributed to the victory: the Navy and Army anti-aircraft gunners, for instance, who shot at nearly every aircraft as a matter of course irrespective of its nationality. The Luftwaffe too had its own problems; most of its bombers were still operating from bases in Germany, and on several occasions much of its effort was diverted to supporting the Wehrmacht's operations elsewhere in France. The Germans had also overestimated the destructive power of bombing, and in particular wasted part of their effort bombing the beaches, where the sand absorbed much of the blast, rather than concentrating on the more vulnerable and important shipping. The persistent cloud cover and variable visibility hindered the bombers, though it also helped to hide their activities from patrolling RAF fighters. One RAF fighter pilot has described his frustration after being shot down at Dunkirk: 'It was very interesting watching things from the ground as I could see the difficulties the fighters are [*sic*] up against. At times we could see Hun bombers bombing from the cloud, while our fighters were about half a mile away obviously unable to see them. The troops could not understand that one could see an aircraft in thin cloud above one, but from the air one could not. One day while we were on patrol, I could see bombs bursting near a destroyer but I could not find the bomber as he was in thin cloud.'* On 30 May though, the cloud and poor visibility prevented the bombers from operating, and on at least two afternoons during the battle a deterioration in visibility saved the shipping from more concentrated assaults.

Perhaps as important as the reasons for the Luftwaffe's failure were the lessons the pilots and commanders of Fighter Command absorbed during the fighting. The pilots learned again the importance of height and the dangers of the 'Hun in the Sun'. They learnt too of the speed of modern air combat, and that despite this the dog-fight was not, as some had predicted, a thing of the past.

The commanders took the opportunity to try out some of the tactics they had been evolving: in particular it was over Dunkirk that the practice of using the Spitfire squadrons to take on the high-flying fighter escorts, whilst the Hurricanes attacked the bombers, was first tried. It is also interesting, in view of the controversy about 'Big Wings' during and after the Battle of Britain, to find that Park was perfectly willing to use his Spitfires and Hurricanes in wing strength at Dunkirk when the circumstances were right. In other words, when there was time to get the aircraft airborne and formed up before coming into contact with the enemy — something which was not possible in 11 Group during the Battle of Britain.

Royal Air Force fighters operating over Dunkirk in 1940 were out of range of the United Kingdom radio and radar control system, and could not therefore be so closely controlled by the sector operations rooms as they were in the Battle of Britain. Furthermore, because of production problems, the British

---

*Pilot Officer R.A.L. Morant, 222 Squadron. Quoted in N. Franks; *The Air Battle of Dunkirk* (William Kimber, 1983) p. 142.

fighters were equipped with the older TR9D radio sets, which were markedly inferior to the latest VHF sets, which did not enter general service until September. In the words of one 41 Squadron pilot: 'We found the communications with Hornchurch when over the Channel quite nil as I remember. We were usually high cover with the Hurricanes well below on low cover.'* Once combat was joined the wing formations rapidly broke up and it became very much a case of every man for himself, most especially since pilots seldom seemed to be able to communicate with aircraft from other squadrons.

Nevertheless Park's use of larger formations — his switch from a policy of weak formations providing continuous cover to one of strong formations with inevitable gaps in the cover provided — while it undoubtedly offered the Germans a free hand for short periods, did reduce the odds against the RAF formations and thus went some way to reducing casualties. Park himself flew his personal Hurricane over Dunkirk and visited operational stations to discover the views of his pilots. In general their comments about the unwieldy nature of wing formations and the problems of controlling them may well have influenced his later tactics in the Battle of Britain.

Dunkirk, as the first major test of the Spitfire in combat with the Luftwaffe fighters, was of the utmost importance and significance from a number of viewpoints. It demonstrated, in the most practical and unarguable fashion, the immense importance of the Spitfire's superior performance in speed, rate of climb and turning circle, as compared with the Hurricane. It dispelled, once and for all, any lingering ideas there might have been that the difference in fighting performance between the two aeroplanes was marginal and of no great significance. Mitchell's uncompromising search for performance in his design was finally justified.

Furthermore, the RAF's Spitfire pilots gained invaluable experience of combat with the Luftwaffe's Messerschmitt Bf 109 and Bf 110. In particular they learnt that the latter, while formidably armed, was no match for a Spitfire; and Bf 110s over Dunkirk were often forced into flying in defensive 'circle' formations; a portent of their relative failure in the Battle of Britain. The RAF pilots also learnt that, properly handled, the Spitfire could outfight, and in particular turn inside, the Bf 109. Equally, they were also quick to appreciate some of the qualities of Willi Messerschmitt's single-seater, especially the advantage bestowed in the dive by the fuel injection system on the German aircraft. These lessons, already suspected after earlier tests on a captured 109, were to be of fundamental importance during the Battle of Britain.

The Spitfire's performance at Dunkirk, both real and imagined, did much to secure the fighter's future, and from that time on it never really looked back.

---

*Pilot Officer E.A. Shipman. Quoted in N. Franks: *The Air Battle of Dunkirk* (William Kimber, 1983) P. 188.

CHAPTER 23

The Battle of Britain

The Battle of Britain was a very public affair. It was fought largely over southern and south-eastern England in full view of the populace who thus had an acute sense of personal involvement, particularly as often enough they were on the receiving end of enemy bombs.

Many words have been written about the Battle by historians, by pilots who fought in it and by senior commanders, and various interpretations have been put upon it. None however can have greater authority than words written by the great Commander-in-Chief of the Royal Air Force, Fighter Command, Air Chief Marshal Sir Hugh C.T. Dowding, GCB, GCVO, CMG, ADC (later created the first Baron Dowding) who not only exercised overall command during the whole period of the battle but who, as the first Commander-in-Chief of Fighter Command, appointed on 14 July 1936, had built up and inspired the fighter force and the control and command system which enabled the battle to be won.

His official dispatch, published in the *London Gazette* in September 1946, contains the following passages:

> The Battle may be said to have started when the Germans had disposed of the French resistance in the summer of 1940, and turned their attention to this country.
>
> The essence of their strategy was so to weaken our fighter defences that their air arm should be able to give adequate support to an attempted invasion of the British Isles . . .
>
> The air supremacy was doubly necessary to them in attacking England because the bulk of their troops and war material must necessarily be conveyed by sea, and, in order to achieve success, they must be capable of giving air protection to the passage and the landing of troops and material.
>
> The destruction or paralysis of the Fighter Command was therefore an essential pre-requisite to the invasion of these Islands.

That succinctly sums up what the Battle of Britain was all about. It is a matter of history that the Germans failed in their objective of the 'destruction or paralysis of the Fighter Command' and so the German invasion plan — Operation Sea Lion — had to be called off.

The Order of the Battle of Fighter Command at 8 July 1940 — and Dowding defines 10 July as the opening date of the Battle — comprised 20 squadrons of Spitfires and 22 squadrons of Hurricanes all classed as operational. To those must be added 2

The Commanders.
Air Marshal Sir Hugh (later Lord) Dowding. Commander in Chief Fighter Command in the Battle of Britain

squadrons of Defiants and 7 squadrons of Blenheim fighters, also operational.

Classed as non-operational or in process of forming or re-forming were a further 8 squadrons of Hurricanes.

In No. 11 Group, which covered south-east England and can perhaps be defined roughly as the first line of defence, there were 12 squadrons of Hurricanes and 6 of Spitfires, giving a ratio of 2 to 1 in favour of the Hurricane.

By the end of the Battle, and as at 3 November 1940, the Order of Battle had increased from a total of 52 squadrons to 69 operational squadrons. Among these the ratio of Hurricanes to Spitfires was 38 to 19 (exactly 2 to 1) to which must be added 6 squadrons of Blenheims, 2 of Defiants and 1 of Gladiators.

The Spitfire and the Hurricane differed in many important respects, but they had two essential things in common: both were armed with 8 Browning .303 calibre machine-guns and both were powered with the magnificent Rolls-Royce Merlin engine.

Although they were very different aeroplanes they complemented each other ideally, and it took them both to win the Battle.

In scale the Battle of Britain was small by comparison with air operations which took place in the course of later campaigns of the war, but its effects were enormous. The morale of the British people was uplifted to an extent which enabled them to respond to the positive leadership of Winston Churchill and his coalition government; the effect on opinion in the USA was substantial and greatly strengthened Roosevelt's political hand in providing aid to Britain on a scale which stretched neutrality

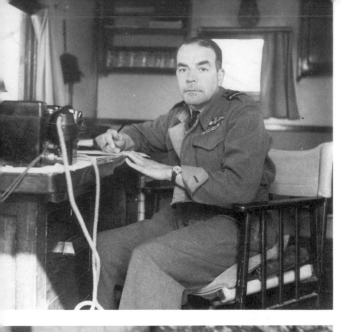

to the limit. It convinced Hitler that he could not eliminate Britain by invasion. It also had a powerful effect in the Commonwealth countries who had instantly committed themselves to the support of Britain on the outbreak of war in 1939 only to witness a series of military reverses and disasters until suddenly the RAF achieved this decisive victory. From 10 July to 31 October, which is deemed officially to be the period of the Battle, a total of 2,945 aircrew fought, out of which 507 were killed and approximately 500 wounded.

This compares with 15,000 British and Allied troops lost in one day at Waterloo. Perhaps aerial warfare is economical in lives, provided it achieves really important strategic objectives.

During the months of July to October (inclusive) the combined output of Spitfire and Hurricane was 1,653 of which 1,025 were Hurricanes and 628 Spitfires. In June the ratio of Hurricanes to Spitfire deliveries had been exactly 3 to 1, but for the four months July to October inclusive Spitfire production increased considerably so that the ratio ran at around 1.6 to 1. This figure gives a fair assessment of the relative numerical participation of those two aircraft in the Battle. Surprisingly British fighter output in this period exeeded that of Germany by a considerable margin. Sir Maurice Dean, KCB, KCMG, in *The Royal Air Force and Two World Wars*,* writes: 'The number of fighters available for operations in Fighter Command rose steadily throughout June, July, August and September. Of course, Fighter Command was too small; not surprisingly surely after years of financial stringency and the collapse of France but, given this qualification, aircraft were not the most severe problem. This arose partly from a shortage of pilots and partly from the vulnerability of fighter and radar stations to attack.'

Apart from the broad strategic issues, what were the special circumstances which affected the Battle? First, the fact that German forces had overrun The Netherlands, Belgium and northern France meant that the Luftwaffe, which was primarily a tactical Air Force having no heavy long-range bomber force to speak of, now had airfields within easy reach of south-eastern England and London which could then be attacked by its medium bombers. Furthermore these bombers could be escorted by high-performance fighters, thereby greatly compounding the problem of Fighter Command in mounting an effective defence.

The second vital circumstance was the availability to the British of a fighter control system based on a chain of radar (with the cover name RDF — radio direction finding) stations. The practical effect of these was that incoming raids could be spotted at a considerable distance from our shores, thus providing essential early warning; the strength of the enemy formations could be assessed wtih reasonable accuracy, and their position, height and track plotted. Not only did this enable the

---

*Cassell, 1979.

British fighters to be controlled or vectored towards their targets by the controllers on the ground but it contributed greatly towards economy of force in that fighters could generally be kept at readiness on the ground until an attack was positively observed. The development of radar stations was a breakthrough of incalculable value but almost as important was the fact that the Luftwaffe High Command had failed to appreciate its significance and was taken largely by surprise. Even if, as has often been claimed, their Intelligence may have been aware of it, the Luftwaffe High Command appears to have failed to benefit from the information. Perhaps this was because German Intelligence was somewhat in disarray due to the rivalry between the Abwehr and the SS, which meant that available information was not always presented in a coordinated manner.

Thirdly, there were the British fighters. The Hurricane and the Spitfire ideally complemented each other. The Hurricane had been designed with ease of production very much in mind; it was rugged and more easily maintained than the Spitfire, and was thus available in greater numbers, but some performance had been sacrificed for these qualities. The Spitfire had a significant edge over the Hurricane in performance which made it more suitable for tackling the German fighters which escorted the bombers. Neither the Spitfire nor the Hurricane could have won the Battle on their own because, apart from anything else, there would not have been enough of them. It took both of these great aeroplanes to win the Battle. Both should always be honoured for the great fighters they were.

Fourthly, there was the aggressiveness and determination of the aircrew in Fighter Command. By and large the pilots had the advantage of fighting over their own country in defence of their own homeland. In the case of the pilots from the Dominions the 'old country' still had a very real meaning and significance for them and they were determined to fight for it. In the case of the foreign pilots — Free Frenchmen, Belgians, Dutch, Poles, Czechoslovaks and Norwegians — they had the stimulus of extreme anger arising from how their own countries had been overrun. A strong element of anger influenced the British pilots as well. Although it is not fashionable to talk about it today, those of us who fought believed we were fighting a just war against unprovoked aggression with Right entirely on our side. We had seen enough of the pre-war Nazi regime to believe it was evil and dangerous and although we were by no means sure it could be beaten, not to fight against it was unthinkable.

The RAF had yet a fifth advantage over the Luftwaffe: it was far better commanded. In 1918 the RAF had been the largest air force in the world in numbers of aircraft, in squadrons and in manpower and it was backed up by the largest and most powerful aircraft industry in the world. At the conclusion of that war the RAF had been run down to a shadow of its former self and had existed on very short rations financially until around 1935. But it was never destroyed, it never went out of business, and indeed the best of it was preserved throughout

TOP LEFT: *Group Captain 'Sailor' Malan*

TOP RIGHT: *Squadron Leader Alan Deere (later Air Commodore)*

CENTRE LEFT: *Lieutenant Pierre Closterman (later Capitaine) – left*

CENTRE RIGHT: *Wing Commander P. G. Jameson (later Air Commodore)*

BOTTOM LEFT: *Squadron Leader C. R. Caldwell*

BOTTOM RIGHT: *Pilot Officer G. F. 'Screwball' Beurling*

the lean years; it also had a world-wide role between the wars. Formed as it was from the old Royal Naval Air Service and the Royal Flying Corps it had absorbed many of the best traditions and habits of command of the older Services. In 1939, therefore, the RAF was a mature service with the priceless asset of having senior officers with the experience and maturity gained from long and uninterrupted service to the Crown.

The German Air Force had had no such luck. Completely dismantled after the war in 1918, its officer corps was disbanded

Rearming and refuelling Spitfire Is during the Battle of Britain. A quick turn-round in those urgent times was vital

and scattered at random over the chaos and despair of post-war Germany. But in fact the German Air Force was never quite out of business – General Hans von Seeckt, Commander of the Reichswehr from 1920 to 1926, had seen to that. Using every possible device and subterfuge to thwart the Versailles Treaty, he kept a tiny cadre of officers and the basis of a planning staff alive and training took place secretly in Russia. The basis of an aircraft industry was created, under the guise of developing civil aircraft within the very limiting terms of the Treaty. The German Air Force, in short, beaten, destroyed and dismantled in 1918, refused to lie down although it may have feigned dead. In the 1920s enormous encouragement and support was given to gliding clubs and thousands of young Germans were able to take this first step towards flying. But it needed a major political upheaval and a direct defiance of the Versailles Treaty before anything like a new Air Force could be created. Hitler provided these conditions and the Luftwaffe was the result. It was in fact an amazing achievement to create a new Air Force, with the industry to back it, on such a scale and in such a short time. But its fundamental weakness was that it was the child of an aggressive political dream and of the appalling corruption of the Nazi party. In such circumstances the command structure of the Luftwaffe was bound to lack mature experience and training in spite of the often valiant and courageous efforts of officers of an older school. This was how the Luftwaffe had to fight the Battle of Britain. It is not surprising that it failed in its first confrontation with a large and really professional air force fighting in defence of its own country.*

The outcome of the Battle had a profound effect upon the British people. The issue had been starkly clear and understandable to all.

Victory for the Luftwaffe was an essential pre-requisite to a German invasion of Britain, which in the depleted state of the army following the disastrous campaigns in France and Belgium, might well have been successful, if costly.

It has been well said that the Battle marked the point when Britain stopped losing the war and was able to move, however slowly and painfully and at whatever cost in blood and treasure, towards eventual victory. The participation of so many pilots from the Empire and from already overrun European countries such as France, Poland and Czechoslovakia, and volunteers from the United States, was symbolic of the fact that Britain was not entirely alone and never would be. There was an heroic dimension, redolent of Horatius and his companions holding the narrow bridge to Rome, which was recognizable to all.

Both the Hurricane and the Spitfire have rightly become part of the folklore of Britain and after so many years have passed are still greeted with affectionate applause by the crowds of a later generation whenever they appear at public air shows.

---

*Spitfire: A Test Pilot's Story, Jeffrey Quill (John Murray, 1983).

The Quantum Jumps

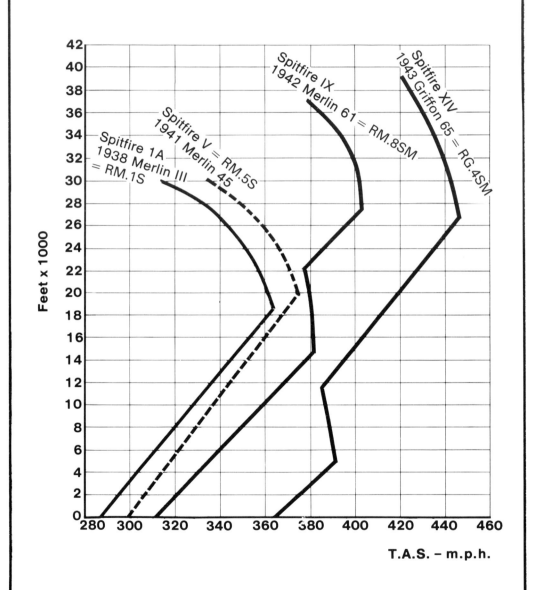

Feet x 1000

Spitfire 1A
1938 Merlin III
= RM.1S

Spitfire V = RM.5S
1941 Merlin 45

Spitfire IX
1942 Merlin 61 = RM.8SM

Spitfire XIV
1943 Griffon 65 = RG.4SM

T.A.S. – m.p.h.

Level Speed Performance

True Airspeeds/Height (m.p.h./feet) A & A.E.E. figures

Spitfire I	5,840 lb
Spitfire V	6,450 lb
Spitfire IX	7,480 lb
Spitfire XIV	7,980 lb
Spitfire 21	8,670 lb
Typhoon 1B	10,540 lb
Tempest V	10,900 lb
P47 Thunderbolt	12,700 lb
Mustang III	8,740 lb

Dates indicate Entry into Service
and operations in Europe

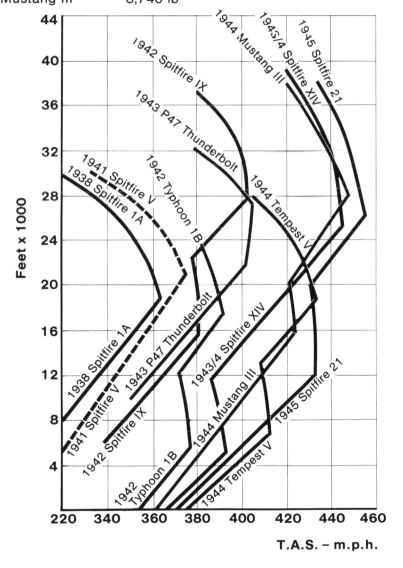

CHAPTER 24

The Spitfire and its Contemporaries

Because it remained in full production and front-line service until the war was over, thus, with the Hurricane, becoming the only fighter on the Allied side to serve from the first to the last day of hostilities, it overlapped with other Allied fighters which were designed and produced a good deal later.

Most of these fighters had very different characteristics and direct comparisons are difficult and complex and must be approached with caution. However, a good basis for comparison is true airspeed plotted against height, in level flight at the combat ratings of the engines.

The Level Speed Performance table (p. 135) is taken from official test data obtained from reports of the Aeroplane and Armament Experimental Establishment at Boscombe Down. These are therefore officially measured figures in each case. The dates shown against each curve represent the year in which the particular aircraft entered operational service in the European theatre of war.

It will be clear from this that from 1938 to 1944 the Spitfire was ahead of all comers at the high and medium-high altitudes. The advent of the Merlin-engined Mustang in 1943–44 pushed the Spitfire IX back into second place, but by then the Spitfire XIV, which in speed ran neck and neck with the Mustang, was already in squadron service.

In speed at low altitude the Tempest V, which came into operational service in 1944, was supreme. In 1942 the Typhoon was the fastest at low altitude. Both Typhoon and Tempest carried very formidable loads of air-to-ground weapons and they were both robust aircraft and probably the best ground attack and 'tank-busting' aircraft on the Allied side.

It has often been said (although I have not checked the arithmetic) that the Typhoon armed with 60lb RPs could loose off a broadside equivalent to that of a 6-inch naval cruiser. These two aircraft came into their own in the vital fighter-ground-attack roles before and after D-Day in Europe, and did a fine job. However, in high-altitude performance the Spitfire left them standing. The Spitfire also, incidentally, developed a useful ground attack capability, but never so formidable as the Typhoon or the Tempest.

However, the point has been made by a distinguished fighter pilot* who did much ground attack work that once the Spitfire

---

*Group Captain Duncan Smith.

had released its bombs or rockets at a ground target it was at once back in business as a high performance and highly manoeuvrable combat fighter.

The Merlin-engined P.51B Mustang which came into operational service at the end of 1943 was a very fine aircraft indeed. It carried a greater load of fuel than the Spitfire and so had a longer operational radius of action. This, combined with its very good altitude performance, made it a first-class escort fighter for daylight bombing raids, and it came into its own in this role in December 1943 and throughout 1944 and 1945 during the massive daylight offensives by the US Air Force.

As a matter of interest the Mustang was designed at North American Aviation to a British specification and built in response to a British contract placed with the approval of the US Government in 1940. The aircraft was originally fitted with an Allison 12-cylinder liquid-cooled engine and its performance, especially at altitude, was disappointing, with the result that in the RAF it was used, from 1942 onwards, in the low-level tactical reconnaissance role. However, its disappointing performance was primarily attributable to its engine and in 1942 a Mustang was fitted experimentally at Hucknall with the Rolls-Royce Merlin 65 engine with 2-stage supercharger and intercooler, the engine which had produced such a spectacular quantum jump in the performance of the Spitfire Mk IX. This turned the Merlin Mustang into one of the finest Allied fighters of the war. Its already substantial fuel capacity allied with its new-found altitude performance made it a natural for the daylight bomber escort role.

In general it can be concluded that the Typhoon and Tempest of 1942 and 1944 were better and more formidable ground attack fighters than the Spitfire was; it can also be concluded that the Mustang was superior as a long-range escort fighter to the Spitfire. Equally it is certain that the Spitfire remained supreme among Allied fighters in the air superiority and air combat roles. Further, it extended its role capabilities to embrace long-range strategic photo-reconnaissance, fighter-reconnaissance, and carrier-based operations in the naval fighter role, as well as its very useful ground attack capability previously mentioned.

Perhaps the one respect in which Spitfire development failed, or was disappointing, was in the full extension of its operational radius of action as a fighter. This prevented it from playing a full part as a long-range escort fighter capable of accompanying the massive American daylight bombing raids deep into enemy territory which became such a feature of the later stages of the war in Europe. Here the Spitfire had to concede pride of place to the Merlin-engined P.51B Mustang, and American fighters such as the P.47 Thunderbolt.

From the beginning the Spitfire had narrow stability margins which meant that it could tolerate only relatively small movements of its centre of gravity during flight.

The radius of action of the photographic-reconnaissance Spitfires from the PR Mk. IV onwards was very greatly extended by converting the whole of the leading edge section of the wings into an integral fuel tank thereby roughly doubling the internal

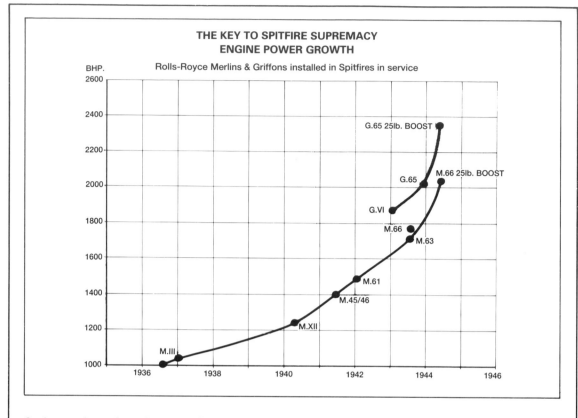

THE KEY TO SPITFIRE SUPREMACY
ENGINE POWER GROWTH

Rolls-Royce Merlins & Griffons installed in Spitfires in service

fuel capacity. Thus the extra fuel was accommodated more or less on the longitudinal centre of gravity and the stability problem did not arise.

The result was that the PR Spitfires were very long-range aircraft penetrating often enough from Benson in Oxfordshire to targets as far distant as Munich and Peenemunde in East Prussia. However this was only achieved at the expense of the wing armament and the PR Spitfires flew totally unarmed relying upon their speed and height for protection.

For the fighters however with their main armament in the wings, the only available space for substantial extra internal tankage was in the fuselage behind the pilot, which resulted in a large rearward movement of the centre of gravity, and so caused considerable stability problems. In fact very marginal longitudinal stability was one of the principal handling problems of the Spitfire throughout its development history and although a great deal of progress was made Supermarine never succeeded in turning it into a really long-range escort fighter. However given a little more time and respite from the massive pressures of wartime production* it would have been done because the problems were well on the way to solution when the war ended.

---

*At one period the combined production of Spitfires and Seafires from Supermarine, Castle Bromwich, Westland and Cunliffe Owen was between 450 and 500 a month.

The two principal German adversaries with which the Spitfire had to contend, in fighter-to-fighter combats, were the Messerschmitt Bf. 109 and the Focke-Wulf FW 190. Like the Spitfire, both these aircraft were developed through various Marks with engines of various power increments and some changes of armament.

Comparisons are therefore difficult and must take into account which Mark of Spitfire is being compared with which Mark of Bf. 109 or FW 190. For example: a Bf. 109 G (1941) would outperform a Spitfire Mk I but certainly not a Spitfire Mk IX, and was on pretty well equal terms with a Spitfire V.

The major early fighter confrontations came at the time of Dunkirk and the Battle of Britain and here the fighting was between the Spitfire Mks. I and II and the Bf. 109 E with Daimler-Benz DB 601A engine.

Much has been written about these operations not only by pilots who fought but also by later historians who drew upon original sources as well as upon each other. This has resulted in some glorious generalities on the subject of aircraft comparative performances, unsupported in most cases by properly measured and established performance figures. It has been well said that history seldom repeats itself, but that historians constantly repeat each other. Thus do misapprehensions proliferate and myths become established.

In the heat, excitement and sometimes confusion of mortal air combat it was very difficult for a pilot to assess calmly the relative performance of his own aircraft against that of his enemy unless the differences were very great.

In an individual air combat, which was virtually a duel to the death between one pilot and another, there was a great deal of chance and circumstance. Things happened quickly and suddenly, men's lives were at stake and impressions were fleeting, sharply emphasized and often unforgettable. Circumstances were never the same, the balance of advantage being with one or other of the combatants from the outset. One had a height or speed advantage — one was up-sun of the other — one achieved surprise and 'bounced' the other — and so on. Impressions of the relative performance and capabilities of the two aircraft concerned were thus strongly influenced by these factors, especially when their performances were fairly closely matched anyway.

So a good number of conflicting stories or impressions have gained currency over the years. There have been writers who, on what they believe to be reliable authority, have stated firmly that in the Battle of Britain the Bf. 109 was superior to the Spitfire in speed and rate of climb below 20,000 feet, others that it was superior above 20,000 feet, others that it was inferior at all heights, and so on.

About the only points on which all are agreed is that the Spitfire had a better turning and manoeuvre performance at all heights, and that at the time of the Battle of Britain the Bf. 109 had one special advantage in manoeuvre over the Spitfire and Hurricane in that its engine did not cut out when subjected to negative 'G'.

My brief experience in fighting against the Bf. 109 E in a

Spitfire Mk. I was mostly around or above 20,000 feet and led me to the conclusion that the Spitfire was slightly superior both in speed and rate of climb, that it was a more 'slippery' or lower drag aeroplane, and that it was outstandingly better in turning circle.

Because of the characteristics of the supercharger of the DB 601 engine I am disposed to accept that the Bf. 109 E may have had a slight edge over the Spitfire in rate of climb somewhere between ground level and 20,000 feet, but there is no real evidence to support an oft-repeated claim that it had a substantially higher rate of climb above 20,000 feet.

However, it is a measured fact that the Bf. 109 generated its optimum rate of climb at a considerably lower forward airspeed than the Spitfire. This meant that at any height the Bf. 109, when at its best climbing speed, would be following a steeper trajectory than the Spitfire at its best climbing speed, although the latter might well be gaining height faster. In certain circumstances there could be a definite tactical significance in this and it might also be visually misleading to an opposing pilot. However impressions gained by pilots in combat or under operational conditions must inevitably have been so much influenced by the circumstances and pressures of the moment that they were essentially subjective.

The following table of figures, taken from a post-war German source, are probably pretty reliable. Certainly the figures given for the Spitfire align closely with official A & AEE and Supermarine data.

Bf 109E versus British fighters

Aircraft	Engine	Max speed (mph)	At FT height (feet)	Corrected BHP at FT height	Maximum speed in mph at:				
					GL	5,000ft	15,000ft	20,000ft	25,000ft
Bf 109 (AUW 5,775 lb)	DB 601	348	17,500	950	283	302	338	343	328
Hurricane I (AUW 6,750 lb)	Merlin III	311	17,500	965	246	264	303	305	290
Hurricane II (AUW 6,800 lb)	Merlin XX	323	21,000	1,075	268	285	314	319	313
Spitfire I (AUW 6,100 lb)	Merlin III	355	18,500	965	282	302	342	351	340

Aircraft	Service Ceiling (100 ft/min)	Operational Ceiling (500 ft/min)	Time to operational ceiling Min	Sec	Rate of climb at 30,000 ft (ft/min)	Time to 30,000 ft Min	Sec	Rate of climb at 25,000 ft (ft/min)	Time to 25,000 ft Min	Sec
Bf 109	35,200 ft	31,900 ft	20	23	740	17	12	1,340	11	39
Hurricane I	35,000 ft	31,400 ft	21	15	660	17	30	1,260	13	12
Hurricane II	37,600 ft	34,900 ft	19	57	1,160	13	20	1,840	9	48
Spitfire 1	37,400 ft	34,000 ft	21	33	1,020	15	42	1,660	11	33

It is noteworthy that the Spitfire I is shown to have a higher operational ceiling than the Bf. 109 and that its advantage in rate of climb is greater at 30,000 feet than at 25,000 feet, indicating that above 25,000 feet the Bf. 109 was beginning to 'run out of steam', which would also be suggested by its lower operational ceiling.

Furthermore there is almost nothing between them in their time to 25,000 feet, but quite a lot in their time to 30,000, which would tend to suggest that the Bf. 109 might have had an advantage in rate of climb somewhere at the lower altitudes between ground level and 20,000 feet.

One thing that is beyond all possible doubt and certainly nothing to do with subjective assessments is that the FW190, when it first began to appear in the skies over northern France towards the end of 1941, had a markedly better performance than the Spitfire Mk V with which Fighter Command was then equipped. Additionally the nature of the operations at that time meant that the air combats were taking place over France, Belgium or Holland and the Spitfires, being based in England, were thus operating at the extreme limits of their radius of action which put them at a severe tactical disadvantage for they were fighting within the tight constraints of their fuel endurance.

Thus the Fighter Command squadrons, in the course of their offensive sweeps and operations escorting daylight bombing raids, had a very difficult time of it in 1941 and early 1942. The problem was solved by the advent of the Spitfire Mk IX with Rolls-Royce Merlin 61 series engine in 1941, which was able to outclimb and usually outmanoeuvre the FW190, at most heights.

Nevertheless the FW190 was never anything other than a very formidable and dangerous adversary. Designed by Kurt Tank, a good deal later than Willi Messerschmitt's Bf. 109, and powered by the BMW 801 radial engine, it was certainly one of the classic fighters of history.

As the war dragged on the Spitfire was progressively and steadily improved in performance, role capability and armament in order to respond to rapidly changing strategic circumstances and operational scenarios. Much the same was done to the German fighters, the Bf. 109 and the FW190, but to a lesser extent and without the same inexorable and steady forward march of improvement.

Engine power growth was the key to improved performance in speed, rate of climb and operational ceiling. The power of the Merlin increased from 1,030 hp in 1939 to 2,050 hp in 1944 and the Griffon engine in the Spitfire XIV gave just short of 2,400 hp in 1944. It was the steady and progressive increase in available horse-power throughout the war (see page 138) that enabled so much to be done with the Spitfire. This power growth was achieved principally by supercharger development and here the contributions of Dr Stanley (later Sir Stanley) Hooker and Mr Geoff Wilde of Rolls-Royce must be mentioned together with that of Cyril Lovesey, the Development Engineer whose main task was to maintain the mechanical integrity and reliability of the engine as the power doubled and the specific dry weight was roughly halved. Arthur Rubbra had overall responsibility for the engine as Chief Designer (Merlin). It is also remarkable that this power growth was achieved almost entirely on 100-octane fuel which had become available in 1940 (the previous fuel being 87 octane) and only when boost pressures were raised to the extraordinarily high figure of plus 25lb for both Merlin and Griffon was it necessary to resort to 'special' fuel known as 150 grade.

The German fighter engines tended to be of larger capacity (and thus heavier) than the Merlins and Griffons. The Daimler-Benz DB 601 was of 39 litres capacity and the BMW.801 of the FW 190 42 litres (as against the 27 litres of the Merlin and the 37 litres of the Griffon). The Bf 109 E of the Battle of Britain had a DB 601A or 1,200 hp with petrol injection and a fluid drive for its supercharger (which gave it an advantage at the lower altitudes. The Bf 109 F which came into service in 1941 had a much improved performance especially at altitude; it had a DB. 601E of 1,350 hp, but its performance was soon matched by the Spitfire V with Merlin 45 engine of 1,250 hp which also entered service in 1941.

The power growths that were achieved with the DB engines were mostly the result of increases in rpm and changes to valves, valve timing and cylinder heads rather than by supercharger development. They also used such devices as nitrous oxide injection and water methanol injection to produce big power boosts over short periods for combat purposes.

The BMW 801 supercharged, air-cooled 14-cylinder double row radial of 42 litres in the FW190 started its operational life at 1,560 hp, which was later increased to 1,700 hp. Eventually improved versions of this engine, the 'E' and 'F', were rated at 2,000 hp and 2,200 hp respectively, but never saw front-line service for 'wartime Germany was unable to procure the necessary machine tools and metal for their production'.*

Again improvements to the BMW 801 in service leaned heavily upon the MW.50 water-alcohol nitrous oxide injection systems to provide short-time power boosts for combat and emergencies. In mid-1944 the 'long-nosed' FW190 D-9 appeared with the liquid-cooled 12-cylinder Jumo 213A engine and represented the highest performance version of the FW 190 to enter Luftwaffe service. Some FW 190s were also produced with Daimler-Benz engines.

When the Spitfire IX with the Merlin 61 first appeared in Fighter Command in mid-1941 it out-performed the FW190 above 25,000 feet, but the 190 still had a slight edge in speed and climb at the low and medium altitudes. This problem was dealt with by a version of the Merlin 61 designated the 66 with its supercharger gear ratios rescheduled so as to produce its maximum power outputs at somewhat more moderate altitudes than the 61, thus evening the balance between the Spitfire IX and the FW190 at the medium altitudes. At the same time the allowable manifold pressures of the Merlin 61 and 66 were increased from plus 15lb to plus 18lb.

---

*Colonel Van Freisen in the *Rolls-Royce Magazine*, December 1984.

Then in 1943 the Spitfire 12 with the single-stage Griffon VI, of 10 litres greater capacity than the Merlin, came into service, albeit in small numbers, in Fighter Command.

The little aeroplane, marvellously agile and manoeuvrable, could handsomely out-perform the 190 at low altitudes up to 15,000 feet, and the following is an interesting account of an engagement between Spitfire XIIs of No. 91 Squadron and a force of FW190 aircraft at low level.

At around 22.00 hours, in the long evening shadows on 25 May 1943, a force of about 15 FW190 fighter bombers slipped across the English Channel at low level for a hit-and-run raid on Folkestone.

The Hawker F.36/34 fighter prototype of the Hurricane, seen at Brooklands where it made its first flight in November 1935. The Hurricane was the Spitfire's companion at arms and greatly distinguished itself in the Battle of Britain and subsequently.

The FW190 had established itself as a great fighter aircraft and the leader of the attack was probably feeling very confident. Close to the sea his only worry came from the speed of the Hawker Typhoons then beginning to overcome their teething problems. The far more numerous Spitfire Vs could be outrun and outclimbed. At high altitude a new mark of the Spitfire was proving a very dangerous opponent, but at low level and in the rapidly fading light a successful interception would not be easy.

However, his confidence was not borne out. Before reaching

the coast the raiders were intercepted by Spitfires which could follow every move of the FW190s and out-perform them in speed and climb. At least five of the German aircraft went down in the Channel and the rest returned to France without bombing their target.

They had been intercepted by 91 Squadron flying the new Spitfire XII, an aeroplane produced rapidly to meet the threat of the low-level FW190. The first Spitfire XIIs were Spitfire V conversions with a modified tail and clipped wings and powered by the new Rolls-Royce Griffon VI engine.*

This story is recounted to illustrate that there was nearly always a Rolls-Royce engine which could provide the Spitfire with the power it needed throughout the full operational height spectrum on a 'horses for courses' basis. The Griffon VI in the Spitfire XII as quoted above, was later developed into the Griffon 65 with large 2-stage 2-speed intercooled supercharger (of similar technology to that developed for the Merlin 61 and 66) which produced the most powerful power unit produced by Rolls-Royce in the war at 2,375 hp.

Fitted in the Spitfire XIV of 1943 it produced a fighter of spectacular performance at both high and low altitude, as indicated by the fact that the Spitfire XIV played a prominent role in catching and destroying the low-flying V.1 flying bombs in 1944 and its recorded high-level performance speaks for itself.

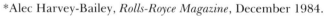

*Alec Harvey-Bailey, *Rolls-Royce Magazine*, December 1984.

Epilogue

"The great immorality open to us in 1940 and 1941 was to lose the war against Hitler's Germany"

(Dr. Noble Frankland in an address to the Royal United Service Institution. December 1961)

In the last analysis when all has been said about the designers, the managers, the administrators, the policy makers, the production organisers and the men and women on the shop floor, the true basis of the Spitfire's legendary aura lay in its contribution to the avoidance of the "great immorality", in the hands of the RAF fighter pilots and their commanders.

In Chapter 23 it was stated that victory in the Battle of Britain marked the point where Britain stopped losing the war and was able to set about winning it, however painfully and at whatever cost in treasure and blood.

By the time the war was won the Royal Air Force had paid a heavy price – 70,253 officers, NCOs and airmen killed or missing of which the overwhelming majority were aircrew.

It had been widely considered that the casualties of World War I had destroyed the flower of a generation, but the total of officers from the entire British Empire who were killed in that war (38,834) was less than the aircrew casualties of Bomber Command alone in the 1939–45 War.

By June 1940 the spectacle of the German army, supported by the Luftwaffe, slicing its way through the low countries and France to Paris and beyond had created amongst the British people a feeling of the invincibility of the Germans and their military equipment, which perhaps had its origins in the unwelcome realisation of the military impotence and unpreparedness of Britain and France which became so apparent in the diplomatic reverses of the immediate pre-war period such as the Rhineland and Munich.

Thus the idea of the superiority of Germany military equipment had become widespread and so it came as a welcome surprise and a blessed relief when suddenly in 1940 it became plain for all to see that the Spitfire could outfight and outmanoeuvre the best fighter that the Germans could put into the battle.

The Spitfire had played no significant part in the Battle of France for Dowding had wisely husbanded his Spitfire force and kept them in this country. Then, at the time of crisis and maximum need, the Royal Air Force had produced, as it were out of the hat, a fighter which was second to none.

From that time onwards the legend was born and kept alive thereafter by the prowess of the fighter pilots who flew Spitfires in combat in every theatre of war, until the end.

Merlin Summary Performance Development

During the period under review the following particulars remained unchanged:

Cubic capacity	27 litres (1 650 cubic inch)
Compresion ratio	6:1
Combat RPM	3 000

	1939	1944
Combat power	Merlin III	Merlin 66
	1 030 HP	2 050 HP
	3 000 RPM	3 000 RPM
	+6¼ lb Boost	+25 lb Boost
Altitude at which engine would give 1 000 HP at a full throttle and 3 000 RPM.	16 000 ft	30 000 ft (Merlin 61 in service June 1942) 36 000 ft (Merlin 113/114)
HP per cubic inch	0.6	1.24
Pounds (net dry) per HP	1.4	0.8
Operating altitudes	Sea level to 32 000 ft	Sea level to 47 000 ft (special Spitfire MK VII, sample production Spitfire IXs flown to 46 000 ft by Alex Henshaw)

Maximum type tested HP (RM17SM, 3 000 RPM + 30lb Boost) — 2 200 HP
Maximum flight clearance tested power (RM17SM) — 2 340 HP
Maximum endurance test power (3 000 RPM + 36 lb Boost, water injection) — 2 640 HP
Longest high power development test, 100 hours at 3 000 RPM + 18lb boost, two successful tests.

APPENDIX 1

Specification F.37/34

This was the Specification tailor made for the Spitfire. The addition of paragraph 6, and especially sub-para (b), is therefore most interesting in the light of Air Marshal Sir Humphrey Edwardes Jones's experience as related in Chapter 15. It should of course be noted that the Rolls-Royce P.V. XII was not evaporatively cooled (paras 2a & d).

The fuel load of 94 gallons (paragraph 3) was subsequently reduced to 75 gallons in order to fit the four extra guns required by Specification F.10/35. Lack of range was subsequently to become one of the Spitfire's few major weaknesses.

CONFIDENTIAL

BRIEF SPECIFICATION FOR HIGH SPEED SINGLE SEATER FIGHTER
(Applicable only to Contract 361140/30/C.4(a))

1. General. This Specification is intended to cover the design and construction of an experimental high speed single seater fighter substantially as described in Supermarine Specification No. 425a and Drawing No. 30000 Sheet 13, except that an improvement in the pilot's view is desirable. The aircraft shall conform to all the requirements stated in Specification No. F.7/30 and all corrigenda thereto except as stated hereunder.

2. Power unit
(a)   The engine to be installed is to be a Rolls-Royce P.V. XII.
(b)   The airscrew shall be of wooden construction and the provisions of paragraph 2(a) of Specification F.7/30 as regards provision for the effect of a metal airscrew on weight and C.G. movement can be ignored.
(c)   The fuel system shall be in accordance with D.T.D. Specification 1004. A duplicated engine driven pump system may be used.
(d)   The cooling system is to be of the evaporative cooling type using wing condensers in association with an auxiliary radiator.
(e)   Hand starting gear only is to be provided for engine starting.

3. Load to be carried
The service load shall be as defined in Specification F.7/30, except for departures which may subsequently be agreed between the contractor and the Director of Technical Development.

The fuel load to be carried is to be 94 gallons with oil appropriate to the endurance implied by this fuel.

4. Equipment and miscellaneous
(a)   Non-standard navigation lights of a type approved by D.T.D. may be fitted, and will be supplied by the Contractor.

(b) The requirement of paragraph 8(a) of Specification F.7/30 that the braking system is to be capable of rapid and easy removal is to be deleted.

(c) The reference to handholes or other aids to handling at the wing tips of paragraph 9(d) of Specification F.7/30 is to be altered to read "Internal provision is to be made for taking holding down guys at the wing tips. Hand holes or grips will not be necessary."

(d) The requirement of paragraph 6 as regards gun installation is modified. All 4 guns may be installed outside the airscrew disc.

(e) A tail wheel is to be fitted if practicable.

The following clause was added at a later date

Containers for catching empty cartridge cases and links ejected by the guns are not required.

5. *Structural strength*

(a) Paragraph 5(b) of Specification F.7/30 is to be altered to read "The alighting gear must be able to withstand an impact at a vertical velocity of 10 feet per second, and at this velocity the load on the alighting gear must not exceed $4\frac{1}{2}$ times the fully loaded weight of the aircraft."

(b) Wheels not conforming to paragraph 5(d) of Specification F.7/30 will be accepted, but the actual size and type proposed must be approved by the Director of Technical Development.

6. *Pre-acceptance test flights*

Prior to the delivery of the aircraft it shall have been certified to the D.T.D. by the Contractors:—

(a) That the aircraft has been subjected by the Contractor's pilot to the following tests:—

1. General Flying Tests in accordance with Aircraft Design Memorandum No. 291.

2. Diving Test in accordance with Aircraft Design Memorandum No. 292.

3. Lateral Stability Tests in accordance with Aircraft Design Memorandum No. 293.

4. Spinning Tests in accordance with Aircraft Design Memorandum No. 294, Part I, Section 2.

5. Aerobatic Flying Tests in accordance with Aircraft Design Memorandum No. 295.

(b) That these tests have shown that the aircraft is safe to be flown by Royal Air Force Pilots.

APPENDIX 2

Specification F.10/35

This was the Specification drawn up as a result of the Operational Requirements Branch's investigations into the lethal density of fire necessary to shoot down a modern bomber aircraft. It reflects very clearly the Air Staff's twin preoccupation with speed and firepower in fighter aircraft. It is, in other words, a Specification for a "Bomber-Destroyer", hence paragraph 6(a), which states that a high degree of manoeuvrability at high speed is not required. Subsequent experience was to prove otherwise, and much time was spent in solving the problem of unduly heavy ailerons at high speed which affected the early Spitfires.

The tentative comments in paragraph 3, concerning the desirability of elevating and traversing guns, are a reflection of the discussions which were taking place in the Air Ministry at this time concerning the tactical application of fighter aircraft. The pros and cons of offset guns, both fixed and moveable, were much discussed by the Air Fighting Committee of the Air Ministry, but such guns were finally and wisely abandoned as impractical in December 1935.

SECRET

SINGLE-ENGINE SINGLE-SEATER DAY & NIGHT FIGHTER
(F.10/35)

1. General
The Air Staff require a single-engine single-seater day and night fighter which can fulfil the following conditions:–
(a) Have a speed in excess of the contemporary bomber of at least 40 m.p.h. at 15,000 ft.
(b) Have a number of forward firing machine guns that can produce the maximum hitting power possible in the short space of time available for one attack. To attain this object it is proposed to mount as many guns as possible and it is considered that eight guns should be provided. The requirements are given in more detail below.

2. Performance
(a) *Speed* The maximum possible and not less than 310 m.p.h. at 15,000 ft. at maximum power with the highest speed possible between 5,000 and 15,000 ft.
(b) *Climb* The best possible to 20,000 ft. but secondary to speed and hitting power.
(c) *Service ceiling* Not less than 30,000 ft. is desirable.
(d) *Endurance* ¼ hour at maximum power at sea level plus 1 hour at maximum power at which engine can be run continuously at 15,000 ft. (This should provide ½ hour at maximum power at which engine can be run continuously, (for climb etc.), plus 1 hour at most economic speed at 15,000 ft. (for patrol), plus ¼ hour at maximum power at 15,000 ft (for attack)). To allow for possible increase in engine power during the life of this aircraft, tankage is to be

provided to cover ¼ hour at maximum power at sea level plus 1¼ hours at maximum power at which engine can be run continuously at 15,000 ft.

(e) *Take off and landing* The aircraft to be capable of taking off and landing over a 50 ft. barrier in a distance of 500 yards.

3. Armament

Not less than 6 guns, but 8 guns are desirable. These should be located outside the airscrew disc. Re-loading in the air is not required and the guns should be fired by electrical or means other than bowden wire.

It is comtemplated that some or all of these guns should be mounted to permit of a degree of elevation and traverse with some form of control from the pilot's seat. Though it is not at present possible to give details, it is desirable that designers should be aware of the possibility of this development, which should not, however, be allowed to delay matters at this stage.

4. Ammunition

300 rounds per gun if eight guns are provided and 400 rounds per gun if only six guns are installed.

5. View

(a) The upper hemisphere must be, so far as possible, unobstructed to the view of the pilot to facilitate search and attack. A good view for formation flying is required, both for formation leader and flank aircraft and for night landing.

(b) A field of view of about 10 downwards from the horizontal line of sight is required for locating the target.

6. Handling

(a) A high degree of manoeuvrability at high speeds is not required but good control at slow speeds is essential.

(b) A minimum alteration of tail trim with variations of throttle settings is required.

(c) The aircraft must be a steady firing platform.

7. Special features and equipment

(a) Enclosed cockpit.

(b) Cockpit heating.

(c) Night flying equipment.

(d) R/T.

(e) Oxygen for 2½ hours.

(f) Guns to be easily accessible on the ground for loading and maintenance.

(g) Retractable undercarriage and tailwheel permissible.

(h) Wheel brakes.

(j) Engine starting – if an electric starter is provided a ground accumulator will be used with a plug-in point on the aircraft, an accumulator for this purpose is not required to be carried in the aircraft. The actual starting must be under control of the pilot. In addition hand turning gear is required.

APPENDIX 3

Expansion Schemes

EXPANSION SCHEME "F"

Scheme "F" was drawn up against the background of continuing German re-armament in the air, and the outbreak of the Italo-Abyssinian War. It provided for an increase in the strength and power of the Air Striking Force (i.e. the "retaliatory" bomber forces), by re-arming all light bomber squadrons with medium bombers, and increasing their initial establishment from 12 to 18 aircraft. The final totals under the Scheme were to be 750 medium bombers; 240 heavy bombers; and 420 fighters. It was under this Scheme that the initial production order for the Spitfire was placed.

Scheme "F"

Number of Squadrons		Number of Aircraft		Total No of RAF Front Line Aircraft
M.A.F.*	Overseas	M.A.F.	Overseas	
124	37	1736	468	2204

Composition of the M.A.F.

Type+	Sqns**	I.E.++	Total A/C	Reserves
F	30(5)	14	420	£50,000,000 allocated to
MB	29	18	522	provide war reserves of
MB	19(11)	12	228	150% of first line strength.
HB	20	12	240	With Sqn. reserves this
TB	2	16	32	meant total reserves of
GR	7	18	126	225% of front line
FB	6	6	36	strength.
AC	11(4)	12	132	
	124 (20)		1736	

Notes
*M.A.F. = Metropolitan Air Force; + F = Fighters, MB = Medium Bombers, HB = Heavy Bombers, TB = Torpedo Bombers; GR = General Reconnaissance Aircraft, FB = Flying Boats, AC = Army Co-operation Aircraft;
** Figures in brackets indicate non-regular squadrons; ++ I.E. = Initial Establishment.

EXPANSION SCHEME "J"

Scheme "J" was the first attempt to produce a Scheme based on calculations of actual strategic tasks and requirements. Total fighter strength was calculated on the location, number, and vulnerability of the targets to be defended. The total fighter strength envisaged rose to 532, but the most dramatic increases were in the bomber forces which increased to a total of 1442 aircraft, including 64 squadrons of heavy bombers totalling 896 aircraft. It was this Scheme which Sir Thomas Inskip attacked in his memorandum of 9th December 1937, and as a result of this the Scheme was amended and became Scheme K.

Scheme "J"

Number of Squadrons		Number of Aircraft		Total No of RAF Front Line Aircraft
M.A.F.	Overseas	M.A.F.	Overseas	
154 +4 T.D.*	45	2331 +56	644	3031

Composition of the M.A.F.

Type	Sqns	I.E.	Total A/C	Reserves
F	38(9)	14	532	War reserves for M.A.F.
MB	26(7)	21	546	squadrons were to be
HB	64	14	896	provided on a scale
TB	—	—	—	sufficient to maintain
GR	9	21	189	front line strength for
FB	6	6	36	sixteen weeks of war
AC	11	12	132	
	154(20)		2331	
TD*	4		56	
	158(20)		2387	

Notes
*T.D. = "Trade Defence" Squadrons – location unspecified.

EXPANSION SCHEME "K"

Scheme "K" was a modified form of Scheme "J", cut down in accordance with Sir Thomas Inskip's suggestions. The bomber programme was cut and related to estimates of German strength in the summer of 1938. The overseas increases proposed in Scheme "J" were dropped, and war reserves were reduced. The total number of fighters remained the same as in the previous Scheme, but the ratio of fighters to bombers was significantly altered in favour of the former.

Scheme "K"

Number of Squadrons		Number of Aircraft		Total No of RAF Front Line Aircraft
M.A.F.	Overseas	M.A.F.	Overseas	
145	39	2305	490	2795

Composition of the M.A.F.

Type	Sqns	I.E.	Total A/C	Reserves
F	38(9)	14	532	Except for fighter and
MB	16	24	384	Trade Protection (i.e.
MB	(3)	16	48	flying boat and general
HB	58	16	928	recce sqns) war reserves
GR	9	21	189	were cut from 16 weeks
GR	(4)	14	56	to 9 weeks for reasons of
FB	6	6	36	financial stringency.
AC	11(4)	12	132	Even these reduced
	145(20)		2305	levels, however, were
				not due to be attained
				before 1941.

Notes
Included an Air Striking Force of 77 Squadrons, 1360 aircraft.

EXPANSION SCHEME "L"

Scheme "L" was produced against the background of the "Anschluss" with Austria. The Initial Establishment of the fighter squadrons was increased from 14 to 16 aircraft, thereby increasing the total number of fighters to 608. It also provided for a larger number of medium bomber squadrons and correspondingly reduced number of heavy bomber squadrons. As finally constituted the Scheme was the first to disregard financial considerations, and was based instead on the productive capacity of the British aircraft industry. It reflected the increasing realisation that war was becoming a distinct possibility.

The Scheme also, however, saw the abandonment of the attempt to achieve parity with the estimated strength of the Luftwaffe. The Air Staff did not like the Scheme, and said so, arguing that a strong bomber force, equal in strength to Germany's, backed by adequate fighter forces and sufficient war reserves of aircraft and trained personnel, was necessary to ensure a sound defence.

Scheme "L"

Number of Squadrons		Number of Aircraft		Total No of RAF Front Line Aircraft
M.A.F.	Overseas	M.A.F.	Overseas	
141	39	2373	490	2863

Composition of the M.A.F.

Type	Sqns	I.E.	Total A/C	Reserves
F	38(9)	16	602	Reserves were to be on
MB	23	24	552	the same scale as under
MB	(3)	16	48	Scheme "K", but would
HB	47	16	752	be available by March
GR	9	21	189	1940.
GR	(4)	14	56	
FB	6	6	36	
AC	11(4)	12	132	
	141(20)		2373	

Notes
Included an Air Striking Force of 77 Squadrons, 1360 aircraft.

EXPANSION SCHEME "M"

Scheme "L" had been approved in April 1938, but the pace of events in Europe soon overtook it and under the stimulus provided by the Munich Crisis Scheme "M" was substituted. This Scheme concentrated on building up the strength of the fighter forces of the M.A.F. to 50 squadrons, which were to be equipped with 800 modern fighters of the Typhoon/ Tornado/Whirlwind types. Parity with German offensive air strength was now expressed in terms of the total tonnage of bombs which could be lifted, and production was thus to be concentrated on the heavy bombers of the Stirling/Halifax/Manchester types.

Scheme "M"

Number of Squadrons		Number of Aircraft		Total No of RAF Front Line Aircraft
M.A.F.	Overseas	M.A.F.	Overseas	
163	49	2549	636	3185

Composition of the M.A.F.

Type	Sqns	I.E.	Total A/C	Reserves
F	50(14)	16	800	The provision of adequate reserves was difficult whilst re-equipment was underway. The broad aim was to provide substantial reserves for fighter sqns. by 1.4.40., and substantial but not complete reserves for bomber sqns by summer 1941.
HB	85	16	1360	
TB/GR	2	21	42	
GR	7	21	147	
GR	(4)	14	56	
GR/FB	6	6	36	
AC	9(2)	12	108	
	163(20)		2549	

Notes
Included an Air Striking Force of 85 Heavy Bomber Squadrons, 1360 aircraft.

APPENDIX 4

Spitfire and Seafire Operational Marks

SPITFIRES: FIGHTERS

Mk I$_A$	1030 hp R.R. Merlin II, III	8 × .303 machine guns
Mk I$_B$	1030 hp R.R. Merlin III	Armed initially with 2 × 20 mm cannon only; later 2 × 20 mm plus 4 rcmg[7]
Mk II$_A$	1175 hp R.R. Merlin XII	Produced at Castle Bromwich
Mk II$_A$ (L.R.)	1175 hp R.R. Merlin XII	Fitted with 90 gal. long range fuel tank under port wing
Mk II$_B$	1175 hp R.R. Merlin XII	Mk II with 'B' Wing – 2 × 20 mm plus 4 rcmg
Mk II$_C$	1175 hp R.R. Merlin XII	Later designated ASR II (Air Sea Rescue)
Mk V$_A$	1470 hp R.R. Merlin XLV (45)	8 rcmg
F.Mk V$_B$	1470 hp R.R. Merlin 45 1415 hp R.R. Merlin 46	'B' Wing Engine with higher rated altitude
L.F.Mk V$_B$	1585 hp R.R. Merlin 45M	Lower altitude rating engine
F.Mk V$_C$	1470 hp R.R. Merlin 45, 50, 50A, 55, 56 1415 hp R.R. Merlin 46	'C' Universal wing
L.F.Mk V$_C$	1585 hp R.R. Merlin 45M, 50M, 55M	Lower altitude rating
Mk VI	1415 hp R.R. Merlin 47	Pressure cabin (PC)
Mk VII	1710 hp R.R. Merlin 64	PC & 2-speed, 2-stage Merlin
F.Mk VIII	1565 hp R.R. Merlin 61 1565 hp R.R. Merlin 61 1650 hp R.R. Merlin 63 1710 hp R.R. Merlin 63A	
L.F.Mk VIII	1580 hp R.R. Merlin 66	
H.F.Mk VIII	1475 hp R.R. Merlin 70	
F.Mk IX$_C$	1565 hp R.R. Merlin 61 1650 hp R.R. Merlin 63 1710 hp R.R. Merlin 63A	
L.F.Mk IX$_C$	1580 hp R.R. Merlin 66	
H.F.Mk IX	1475 hp R.R. Merlin 70	
F.Mk IX$_E$	R.R. Merlin 61, 63, 63A	'B' Wing 2 x 20mm cannon + 2 × 0.5 in. mgs
L.F.Mk IX$_E$	1580 hp R.R. Merlin 66	
H.F.Mk IX$_E$	1475 hp R.R. Merlin 70	
Mk XII	1735 hp R.R. Griffon III, IV	
Mk XIV$_C$	2035 hp R.R. Griffon 65	'C' Wing
F.Mk XIV$_E$	2035 hp R.R. Griffon 65	'E' Wing
F.R.Mk XIV$_E$	2035 hp R.R. Griffon 65	Rear-view fuselage. Oblique camera in rear fuselage
L.F.Mk XVI	1580 hp Packard R.R. Merlin 266	'C' Wing
L.F.Mk XVI$_E$	1580 hp Packard R.R. Merlin 266	'E' Wing
Mk 21	2035 hp R.R. Griffon 61	

SPITFIRES: PHOTO RECONNAISSANCE

Type 'A'	1030 hp R.R. Merlin III	No extra fuel
Type 'B'	1030 hp R.R. Merlin III	Extra 30 gal. tank in fuselage behind pilot
Type 'C'	1030 hp R.R. Merlin III	As 'B' with additional 30 gal. fuel tank under port wing
Type 'D'	1030 hp R.R. Merlin III	Special long range. Leading edge wing tank, + 30 gal. fuselage tank
Type 'F' (PR Mk VI)	1030 hp R.R. Merlin III 1470 hp R.R. Merlin 45	As 'B' with additional 30 gal. tank under each wing
Type 'G' (PR Mk VII)	1030 hp R. R. Merlin III 1470 hp R.R. Merlin 45	Armed low level PR Aircraft
P.R. Mk IV	1470 hp R.R. Merlin 45 1415 hp R.R. Merlin 46	Production version of Type D, fitted with Merlin 45/46
P.R. Mk X	1475 hp R.R. Merlin 77	P.C. 2-stage, 2-speed s/c
P.R. Mk XI	R.R. Merlin 61, 63, 63A, 70	
P.R. Mk XIII	1645 hp R.R. Merlin 32	Armed low level P.R. produced by conversion
P.R. Mk XIX	2035 hp R.R. Griffon 65, 66	All except first 22 with PC
F.Mk VI (P.R.)	1415 hp R.R. Merlin 47	6 Mk VI fighters sent to ME in 1942 for P.R. work

SEAFIRES

Mk IB	1470 hp R.R. Merlin 45 1415 hp R.R. Merlin 46	Produced by conversion from Spitfire VB
Mk IIC	1470 hp R.R. Merlin 45, 50A 1415 hp R.R. Merlin 46	'C' Wing
Mk L.IIC	1645 hp R.R. Merlin 32	
Mk L.R. IIC	1645 hp R.R. Merlin 32	F.R. version of L.IIC
Mk L.IIC (Hybrid)	1585 hp R.R. Merlin 55M	26 basic Mk IIIs produced by Westlands with fixed 'C' Wing
Mk F.III 1470 hp R.R. Merlin 55 Folding 'C' Wings		
Mk L.III	1585 hp R.R. Merlin 55M	
Mk F.R. III	1585 hp R.R. Merlin 55M	
Mk XV	1815 hp R.R. Griffon VI	
Mks F & FRXVII	1815 hp R.R. Griffon VI	
Mks F & FR 47	2145 hp R.R. Griffon 87 2350 hp R.R. Griffon 88	

NOTES

1. Spitfire Mk IIA (L.R.) is an unofficial designation, but is a convenient way of distinguishing the IIA with the extra under wing fuel tank from the standard IIA. Approximately 100 were produced.
2. Spitfires F & F.R. Mk XVIII and Mk 22 did not become operational in the Royal Air Force until after the cessation of hostilities.
3. Spitfire 'P.R. Type E': There was only one known example and I have omitted it from the list.
4. Spitfire F.Mk VI (P.R.). This again is an unofficial designation. These aircraft were soon relegated to communications duties, but two operational sorties took place with 680 (P.R.) Squadron in 1943: one in April to Crete, the other in May to Crete and Piraeus.
5. Seafire XV. This aircraft received its Service Release in April 1945.
6. The Seafires Mk XVII and 47 entered Squadron Service after the cessation of hostilities. The Mk 47 was operational in the Korean War.
7. This stands for rifle calibre machine gun.

Index